Que® Quick Reference Series

1-2-3® Release 2.3 for DOS Quick Reference

Rosemary Colonna

1-2-3® Release 2.3 for DOS Quick Reference.
Copyright © 1991 by Que® Corporation.

Library of Congress Catalog No.: 91-61985
ISBN 0-88022-725-7

93 92 91   6 5 4 3 2 1

Interpretation of the printing code: the rightmost double-digit
number is the year of the book's printing; the rightmost single-
digit number, the number of the book's printing. For example,
a printing code of 91-1 shows that the first printing of the
book occurred in 1991.

This book is based on Release 2.3 of Lotus 1-2-3.

Que Quick Reference Series

The *Que Quick Reference Series* is a portable resource of essential microcomputer knowledge. Drawing on the experience of many of Que's best-selling authors, the Que Quick Reference Series helps you easily access important program information.

The Que Quick Reference Series includes these titles:

1-2-3 Quick Reference
1-2-3 Release 2.3 for DOS Quick Reference
1-2-3 Release 3 Quick Reference
1-2-3 Release 3.1 Quick Reference
Allways Quick Reference
Assembly Language Quick Reference
AutoCAD Quick Reference, 2nd edition
C Quick Reference
CorelDRAW Quick Reference
dBASE IV Quick Reference
DOS and BIOS Functions Quick Reference
Excel Quick Reference
Hard Disk Quick Reference
Harvard Graphics Quick Reference
MS-DOS Quick Reference
Microsoft Word 5 Quick Reference
Norton Utilities Quick Reference
PC Tools Quick Reference, 2nd Edition
Q&A Quick Reference
QuickBASIC Quick Reference
Quicken Quick Reference
Turbo Pascal Quick Reference
UNIX Programmer's Quick Reference
UNIX Shell Commands Quick Reference
Windows 3 Quick Reference
WordPerfect Quick Reference
WordPerfect 5.1 Quick Reference

Publisher

Lloyd J. Short

Series Director

Karen A. Bluestein

Production Editor

Jo Anna Arnott

Technical Editor

Lynda A. Fox

Production Team

Kimberly Leslie

Trademark Acknowledgments

1-2-3 and Symphony are registered trademarks of Lotus Development Corporation.

EPSON is a registered trademark of Epson America, Inc.

MS-DOS is a registered trademark of Microsoft Corporation.

Composed in Times and Macmillan by Que Corporation

Table of Contents

Introduction

1-2-3 Release 2.3 for DOS Quick Reference is not a rehash of
traditional documentation. Instead, this quick reference is a
compilation of the most frequently used information from
Que's best-selling 1-2-3 books.

1-2-3 Release 2.3 for DOS Quick Reference presents essential
information on 1-2-3 commands, @ functions, and macros.
You learn the proper use of primary 1-2-3 functions and the
new WYSIWYG options that help you enhance your
spreadsheets. *1-2-3 Release 2.3 for DOS Quick Reference*
contains fundamental information in a compact, easy-to-use
format.

Although *1-2-3 Release 2.3 for DOS Quick Reference* contains
essential 1-2-3 information, it is not intended as a replacement
for the comprehensive information presented in a full-size
guide. You should supplement this quick reference with one of
Que's complete 1-2-3 texts, such as *Using 1-2-3 Release 2.3*.

Now you can put essential information at your fingertips with
1-2-3 Release 2.3 for DOS Quick Reference—and the entire
Que Quick Reference Series!

WORKSHEET BASICS

Lotus 1-2-3 is used to perform repetitive math calculations, analyze data, manage files, and draw graphs.

1-2-3 commands are used to perform functions, such as copying or moving portions of the worksheet, formatting cells to display currency, and using the database. You access 1-2-3 commands through a variety of menus. Some menus and commands ask you to enter text or cell-address information. Other prompts request just text. After you supply an answer to a prompt, press **Enter**.

The *command line,* the second line on the screen, shows the current menu selections. To choose a menu item, press →, ←, or the **space bar** until your choice is highlighted, and then press **Enter.** A quicker method is to type the first character of the menu item. If you use the arrow keys to select a menu item, note that the cell pointer "wraps around" the end of the menu line in either direction.

As you use 1-2-3, watch the *prompt line,* which is the third line. If you make an incorrect selection from a menu, you will see an error message in the prompt line. Press **Esc** to back up to the preceding menu.

Pointer Keys

Move the cell pointer in the worksheet, across worksheets in a file, and across active files. Many of the same keys move the cursor in EDIT mode. Use the **Num Lock** key to toggle between pointer movement and 10-key entry.

For a key combination such as **Shift-Tab**, press the first key, and then quickly press the second key. A plus sign between key names means you should press the two keys in turn and not simultaneously.

Pointer Keys with One Worksheet

Key	Function
←	Moves cell pointer left one cell.
→	Moves cell pointer right one cell.
↑	Moves cell pointer up one cell.
↓	Moves cell pointer down one cell.
Ctrl-← or **Shift-Tab**	Moves the cell pointer one screen to the left.
Ctrl-→ or **Tab**	Moves the cell pointer one screen to the right.
End+ ←	Moves the cell pointer to the left.[*]
End+ →	Moves the cell pointer to the right.[*]
End+ ↑	Moves the cell pointer up.[*]
End+ ↓	Moves the cell pointer down.[*]
End+Home	Moves the cell pointer to the lowest right corner of the active area.
Home	Moves the pointer to the upper left corner of the worksheet (cell A1 in normal operation) or to the upper left unfixed cell when titles are fixed with /Worksheet Titles.
Num Lock	Toggles the numeric keypad from pointer movement to numeric entry.
PgUp	Moves cell pointer up one screen.
PgDn	Moves cell pointer down one screen.

Key	Function
F5 (GoTo)	Prompts for a cell address or range name, and then moves the cell pointer directly to that cell.
F6 (Window)	If the window is split, moves the cell pointer to the next window (which can be in another worksheet or file).
Scroll Lock	Toggles the scroll function on and off; when on, moves the entire window when you press one of the four arrow keys.
*	*Moves the cell pointer in the direction of the arrow to the next intersection between a blank cell and a cell that contains data.*

Function Keys

Function keys save time as you perform special tasks. Depending on the hardware, function keys are labeled F1 through F10. Some keyboards have 12 (or more) function keys. 1-2-3 uses only the first 10.

Following is a list of function keys and function-key combinations.

Key	Name	Function
F1	(Help)	Accesses the on-line help facility.
F2	(Edit)	Places 1-2-3 in EDIT mode so that you can change the current cell. If a dialog box is on the screen, and 1-2-3 is in MENU mode, it activates the dialog box.
F3	(Name)	In POINT mode, displays a list of available named ranges. If pressed again, displays a full screen list of named ranges.

Key	Name	Function
		In FILE mode, displays file names. In VALUE mode, after you type + – / ^ (or * in a formula, 1-2-3 displays a menu of named ranges.
F4	(Abs)	Changes a cell or range address from relative to absolute to mixed.
F5	(GoTo)	Moves the cell pointer to a cell address or range name.
F6	(Window)	Moves the cell pointer to another window or worksheet when the screen is split. In Rel. 2.2 and 2.3, toggles between settings sheets and worksheet display. Also turns off the display of settings sheets in MENU mode.
F7	(Query)	Repeats the last /Data Query command.
F8	(Table)	Repeats the last /Data Table command.
F9	(Calc)	In READY mode, recalculates all formulas in the worksheet. If entering or editing a formula, converts the formula to its current value.
F10	(Graph)	Displays the graph defined by the current graph settings.
Alt-F1	(Compose)	Creates international characters that cannot be typed directly with the keyboard.

Key	Name	Function
Alt-F2	(Step)	Single steps through macros for debugging purposes. When pressed again, it turns step mode off.
Alt-F3	(Run)	Runs a macro you select from the list of range names displayed.
Alt-F4	(Undo)	Reverses the last action.
Alt-F5	(Learn)	Turns on the Learn feature so that all keystrokes are recorded into a previously defined worksheet range. This feature is used to create macros. Pressed again, it turns off LEARN mode.
Alt-F7 or **Shift-F7**	(App1)	Starts an add-in application assigned to this key.
Alt-F8 or **Shift-F8**	(App2)	Starts an add-in application assigned to this key.
Alt-F9 or **Shift-F9**	(App3)	Starts an add-in application assigned to this key.
Alt-F10 or **Shift-F10**	(App4)	Starts an add-in application assigned to this key. When no add-in programs are assigned to this key, using it displays the Add-in menu.

Other Special 1-2-3 Keys

Key	Function
Backspace	During cell definition or editing, erases the preceding character. Cancels old ranges shown in some prompts. Displays the preceding Help Screen if you are using Help.

Key	Function
/ (slash)	Starts a command from READY mode. Used as the division symbol when data is entered or a formula is edited in a cell.
. (period)	When used in a range address, separates the address of the cell at the beginning of the range from the address of the cell at the end of the range. In POINT mode, moves the anchor cell to another corner of the range.
Break	Cancels a macro or cancels menu choices and returns to READY mode.
Esc	When accessing the command menus, cancels the current menu and returns to the preceding menu. Returns to READY mode if at the Main menu. Clears the edit line when entering or editing data in a cell. Cancels a range during some prompts that display the old range. Returns from the on-line help facility.

Using a Mouse

You can use a mouse with 1-2-3 Release 2.3 if the mouse driver for your mouse is installed. To install your mouse driver, see the documentation that came with your mouse. When WYSIWYG is loaded into memory, the mouse has additional capabilities, such as changing the column width or row height and editing graphs. To install WYSIWYG, use the procedure outlined in the WYSIWYG section of this book.

Reminders

When you move the mouse pointer to the Control panel, the 1-2-3 Main menu or the WYSIWYG Main menu, whichever you last used, appears. Click the right mouse button to toggle between these menus.

To select icons with the mouse

When you use a mouse, 1-2-3 displays icons in the icon panel located to the right of the worksheet area. You can select icons with the mouse. The icon panel contains the following icons.

◄	Moves the cell pointer left in the current worksheet.
►	Moves the cell pointer right in the current worksheet.
▲	Moves the cell pointer up in the current worksheet.
▼	Moves the cell pointer down in the current worksheet.
?	Displays help.

To move the cell pointer with a mouse

You can move the cell pointer with a mouse as well as with the pointer-movement keys.

To move the cell pointer to a cell with the mouse, click that cell with the left mouse button. To move the cell pointer around the worksheet, position the mouse pointer on top of the cell pointer, press and hold the left mouse button, and move or drag the cell pointer to another location in the worksheet. Release the button. Move the cell pointer by clicking the triangle and arrow icons that appear in the icon panel. Click the triangles with the left mouse button to move the cell pointer in the direction that a triangle points within a worksheet.

To create windows with a mouse

You can use the mouse to create horizontal or vertical windows whenever 1-2-3 is in READY mode and WYSIWYG is in memory.

1. Move the mouse pointer to the upper left corner of the worksheet. Press and hold the left mouse button.

2. To create a horizontal window, drag the mouse pointer down until the window is the size you want. Release the button.

    To create a vertical window, drag the mouse pointer to the right until the window is the size you want. Release the button.

3. To remove the window, select /WWC.

To select menu commands

You can use the mouse to select commands from either the 1-2-3 Main menu or the WYSIWYG Main menu.

1. Move the mouse pointer to the Control panel.

2. Click the command with the left mouse button.

3. To move back to the previous menu, click the right mouse button.

4. If the Worksheet command is highlighted, to return 1-2-3 to READY mode, move the mouse pointer to the worksheet. If it is not highlighted, move the mouse pointer to the worksheet and press the right mouse button until the menus disappear.

To specify a range with a mouse

1. Move the mouse pointer to a corner cell of the range you want to specify.

2. Press and hold the left mouse button to anchor the cell pointer.

3. Drag the mouse pointer to the corner diagonally opposite and release the button.

4. Click the left mouse button to specify the range.

5. To cancel the highlighted range, click the right mouse button.

To highlight a range before selecting a command

You can highlight a range before you select a WYSIWYG command (but not a 1-2-3 Main menu

command). You can use this technique with the
WYSIWYG :Format and :Text commands.

1. Position the cell pointer in one corner of the range
    you want to specify.

2. To anchor the cell pointer, press F4.

3. Click and hold the left mouse button and drag the
    mouse to the opposite corner of the range.

4. Release the button, and then click the left mouse
    button again to accept the range.

5. Type :.

6. Select any WYSIWYG commands that you want
    which require ranges.

7. Select any other commands that you want.

8. Press Esc, move the cell pointer, or click the left
    mouse button when you no longer want to work with
    the range.

To specify files with a mouse

When you select a command that automatically lists
files, such as /File Retrieve, menu items are displayed in
the first line of the control panel.

1. Click any of the following menu items, displayed on
    the top line of the control panel, with the left mouse
    button:

Menu item	Function
List	Displays a full-screen list of subdirectories and files in the current directory on the current drive.
.. (ellipsis)	Lists in the control panel subdirectories and files in the root directory (or the subdirectory above the current directory) that are on the current drive.

Menu item	*Function*
▲ ▼	Moves the menu pointer left, right, up, or down through the displayed list of subdirectories and files.
A: B: C: D:	Replaces the drive letter in the path displayed in the control panel with the drive letter you select, and lists subdirectories and files located on that drive.

2. To specify a file, click the file name with the left mouse button.

Reminder

The drive choice menu item displays only when WYSIWYG is invoked. In order to change the current drive without WYSIWYG, it is necessary to use the right mouse button or the Esc key.

To adjust column width

If you set the display of your worksheet frame with :Display Options Frame Enhanced or :Display Options Frame Relief, you can use the mouse to set the width of a column whenever 1-2-3 is in READY mode.

1. Move the mouse pointer to the vertical line to the right of the column letter of the column you want to adjust.

2. Press and hold the left mouse button.

3. Drag the mouse pointer to the right or left until the column is the width you want and release the button.

To adjust row height

If you set the display of your worksheet frame with :Display Options Frame Enhanced or :Display Options Frame Relief, you can use the mouse to set the height of a row whenever 1-2-3 is in READY mode.

1. Move the mouse pointer to the horizontal line below the row number of the row that you want to adjust.

2. Press and hold the left mouse button.

3. Drag the mouse pointer down until the row is the
    height you want. Release the button.

Notes

You can return to cell A1 from any point in the
worksheet by clicking the upper left corner of the
worksheet frame with the left mouse button.

When the mouse pointer is in the Control panel, you can
scan menu items by pressing and holding the left mouse
button while moving the mouse pointer across the
command line. The mouse pointer highlights each menu
item it touches, and a description or submenu for that
item appears in the third line of the Control panel. You
select the highlighted item when you release the left
button.

If you drag the mouse pointer past the vertical line to the
left of the column letter, and release the button, you can
hide a column. To display a hidden column, click the left
mouse button on the vertical line to the right of the
column letter before the column you want to redisplay.
While holding the button, move the pointer to the right
until the column is the width you want, and then release
the button.

If you drag the mouse pointer up, past the horizontal line
above the row number, and release the button, you will
hide the row. To display a hidden row, click the left
mouse button on the horizontal line below the row
number of the row that is above the row you want to
redisplay. While holding the button, move the pointer
until the row is the height you want, and then release the
button.

Cell and Range Addresses

Purpose

Identify the location of a cell or range.

To type a cell reference

Type the address of the cell (**C12**, for example). For a
range, separate the addresses of the two corners with a

period (**C5.F16**, for example); 1-2-3 inserts the second period automatically.

To include a cell reference by pointing

Use any of the pointer movement keys to select a cell. For a range, press the period to anchor the cell, then point to the opposite corner of the range.

To include a cell reference with range names

Type the range name instead of the cell or range address. Press **F3** (Name) for a list of range names. Select the range name from the list. Press **F3** again for a full-screen list of range names.

Relative and Absolute References

Purpose

Specify how a cell reference in a formula adjusts when it is copied to another cell.

Notes

The default relative references adjust automatically when you copy the formula to another cell. The formula **@SUM(B3..B6)** in cell B8, for example, becomes **@SUM(C15..C18)** when it is copied to cell C20.

Absolute references do not adjust when copied. An absolute address is preceded by a dollar sign ($) in each part of the address, for example, **B3..B6**.

Mixed addresses are both relative and absolute. The relative parts adjust and the absolute parts do not. The absolute part of the address must be preceded by a dollar sign ($). The formula **@SUM(B$3..B$6)** in cell B8 becomes **@SUM(C$3..C$6)** when it is copied to C20.

To make a cell reference absolute, select the cell and press **F4** (Abs). To make the cell reference mixed, press **F4** until the correct combination appears. To make a range name absolute, precede the name with a dollar sign. A range name cannot have a mixed address.

ENTERING AND EDITING DATA

After you type the first character of an entry, 1-2-3 determines the type of entry. If the entry is text, the mode indicator changes to LABEL. If the entry is the beginning of a number or formula, the VALUE mode is activated.

Entering Labels

To enter a label

Type the label into the cell. If the label starts with one of the following numeric characters,

0 1 2 3 4 5 6 7 8 9 . + − $ (@ #

you must precede the label with a label prefix. The label prefix tells 1-2-3 that the entry is a label and indicates how the text is aligned in the cell.

Notes

Following are label prefixes you can use to control alignment:

Label Prefix	*Function*
'(apostrophe)	Aligns label to the left (default setting).
" (quotation mark)	Aligns label to the right.
^ (caret)	Centers label in the cell.

Label Prefix	Function
\ (backslash)	Repeats character to fill a cell.[*]
| (vertical bar)	Aligns label to the left, and does not print it. [*]

[*]This prefix cannot be selected with /WGL or /RL.

You can change the default label prefix with /Worksheet Global Label-Prefix. You may only use this to change new labels. To change the alignment of existing labels, you can use /Range Label.

Entering Numbers

To enter a number

Begin typing with one of the following characters:

0 1 2 3 4 5 6 7 8 9 . + – $

Notes

Numeric formulas operate on numbers, string formulas operate on text, and logical formulas compare two entries. The result of a logical test is TRUE or FALSE. TRUE has a value of 1 and FALSE has a value of 0. The following items can be included in formulas:

Item	Description
@functions	Predefined formulas
Addresses	Cell addresses or range names
Operators	Symbols, such as + and –, for numeric, string, or logical operations
Numbers	Used for math calculations
Strings	Text used in string formulas

Following is a list of numeric operators (the order of precedence is from the top of the list down):

Operator	Meaning
^	Exponentiation (to the power)
+/–	Positive, Negative
*//	Multiplication, Division
+/–	Addition, Subtraction

Following is a list of logical operators:

Operator	Meaning
=/<>	Equal, Not equal
</>	Less than, Greater than
</=	Less than or equal to
>/=	Greater than or equal to
#NOT#	Logical NOT. Reverses a true/false result.
#AND#	Logical AND
#OR#	Logical OR

Following is a list of string operators:

Operator	Function
+	Repeats the string or cell addresses. This operator must be used only once, at the beginning of the formula.
&	Adds a string to the preceding string.

To place a string inside a formula, enclose it in double quotation marks.

Editing Cell Contents

Use the **Backspace** key to correct a typing error. For more extensive changes, press **F2** (Edit).

To write over existing cell contents

Type a new entry; the new entry replaces the old entry when you press **Enter**. To cancel the new entry and keep the old entry, press **Esc** before you press **Enter**.

To edit cell contents

1. Press **F2** (Edit). The cell contents appear on the second line of the screen. The flashing cursor indicates where your typing will be placed.

2. Use the edit keys to make any changes.

3. When you finish editing, press **Enter** (the cursor can be anywhere in the edit line at this time).

1-2-3 COMMAND REFERENCE

The Command Reference includes all the 1-2-3 commands. Each command is presented in the same format: the command name appears first, followed by the keystroke(s) required to activate the command, the purpose of the command, and reminders of any preparation required before activating the command.

Add-In Attach

/AA

Purpose

Loads an add-in application program into memory. Add-in applications are programs that work along with 1-2-3 to extend its capabilities. Rel. 2.3 comes with five add-in programs: Auditor, Macro Library Manager, Tutor, Viewer, and WYSIWYG.

With this command, you assign a function key (such as
Alt-F7) which you can use to invoke the add-in each
time you want to use it.

Reminders

Add-in programs must be located in your default 1-2-3
directory. The extension .ADN indicates an add-in
program.

To load an add-in program into memory

1. Type /AA.

2. Highlight the add-in name in the list of .ADN files
    displayed. Press Enter.

3. Select 7, 8, 9, or 10 to assign the add-in to Alt-F7
    through Alt-F10. No-Key does not assign the add-in
    to any function key; it must be invoked with /Add-In
    Invoke.

Notes

If you want an add-in to attach automatically each time
you start 1-2-3, use /Worksheet Global Default Other
Add-in Set. Be sure to use /Worksheet Global Default
Update to save the setting.

When not enough memory is available to attach an
add-in, the MEMORY FULL error message is displayed.
Depending on the amount of memory or the size of your
worksheet, invoking an add-in may disable the Undo
feature. If you have other add-ins attached, use /Add-in
Detach to remove them from memory, allowing room
for the other add-in. You can exit 1-2-3 and free
memory by removing other memory-resident programs.

Add-In Invoke

/AI

Purpose

Activates an add-in program you previously attached.
Use this command when you want to use the commands
or functions in the add-in program.

Reminders

You must attach the add-in with /Add-in Attach or, if you used /Worksheet Global Default Other Add-in Set, the add-in automatically attaches when you load 1-2-3.

If you did not assign a function key to the add-in

1. Type /AI.

2. Highlight the add-in from the list of attached add-ins. Press Enter.

If you assigned a function key to the add-in

1. Press the Alt-function key combination you assigned to the add-in. If, for example, you assigned the add-in to F7, press Alt-F7 to invoke the add-in.

Notes

Refer to the add-in documentation for specific use instructions.

You can attach and invoke the add-in automatically with the /Worksheet Global Default Other Add-in Set command. Answer Yes to the prompt Automatically invoke this add-in when you start 1-2-3. Be sure that you use /Worksheet Global Default Update to save the setting.

Add-In Detach/Clear

/AD or /AC

Purpose

Removes add-ins from memory to free more memory for spreadsheets or other add-ins.

Reminders

You must attach the add-in with /Add-in Attach or, if you used /Worksheet Global Default Other Add-in Set, the add-in is attached automatically when 1-2-3 is loaded.

To remove an add-in from memory

1. Type /AD.

2. Highlight the attached add-in from the displayed list.
   Press Enter.

3. Select Quit to leave the Add-in menu.

To remove all add-ins from memory

1. Type /AC.

2. Select Quit to leave the Add-in menu.

Note

The /AD and /AC commands remove the applications
from memory during the current work session only. If
you have an auto-attached add-in that you no longer
want, use /Worksheet Global Default Other Add-in
Cancel. Be sure to use /Worksheet Global Default
Update to save the setting.

Auditor

Purpose

Auditor is one of the add-in programs that come with
Release 2.3. Enables you to analyze and identify formula
contents in a worksheet and display the information
on-screen.

Reminder

Auditor must be attached (using /Add-In Invoke) before
you can use it. Formula relationships can be set up in
Auditor by using Highlight (highlighting cells), List
(listing cell contents in the worksheet), or Trace (moving
the cell pointer forward or backward to display the next
or previous formula.

To use Auditor

1. Type /Add-in Invoke.

2. Highlight Auditor and press Enter.

3. Select one of the following menu items to perform
   the function you want to use:

Menu Item	*Function*
Precedents	Used to identify all cell contents in the Audit-Range that provide data for a specified formula cell. These cells are required by the formula to calculate a formula result. For this reason, only formulas can have precedents.
Dependents	Used to identify all formula cells in a specified Audit-Range that refer to a particular cell. Best used to see whether a particular cell is referenced by or is dependent on a formula.
Formulas	Searches column-by-column to identify all formula cells in the Audit-Range including file-linking formula cells.
Circs	Identifies all cell contents used in a circular reference and lists their addresses. Can occur in only Natural recalculation when a formula refers to itself either directly or indirectly.
Recalc-List	Provides a list of all worksheet formula cells, except file-linking formula cells, in the order of the method of recalculation specified for the current worksheet (Natural, Columnwise, or Rowwise).
Options	Lets you modify default settings to select the mode in which Auditor identifies precedents, dependents,

Menu Item	*Function*
Options (cont.)	formulas, recalculation lists, and circular references. Also provides a means to return to default settings. Choose from the following menu items:

Highlight. The default audit mode that displays particular cells in bright intensity or in a different color (if you have a color monitor) enabling you to examine relationships among highlighted cells.

List. An audit mode that creates a list of precedent, dependent, circular reference, or formula cells identified by the Auditor, in a specified range, showing their contents.

Trace. An audit mode that enables you to locate cells identified by the Auditor by letting you move the cell pointer. Hidden columns are displayed in Trace mode.

Audit-Range. The method you use to specify the range to audit to find precedent, dependent, or formula cells.

Reset. Used to reset the Auditor settings to the default (Audit-Range to A1..IV8192) or to remove the highlight from highlighted cells, and then return the Auditor to the previous menu.

Quit. Returns you to the Auditor main menu.

Menu Item	*Function*
Quit	Returns 1-2-3 to READY mode, keeping the Auditor add-in attached until you either leave the 1-2-3 session or use /Add-in Detach or /Add-in Clear.

Note

Auditor will not write over any existing data in the specified output range—the list output range must be blank.

Copy

/C

Purpose

Copies formulas, values, labels, formats, and cell-protection attributes to new locations.

Reminders

Make sure that you have enough space on your worksheets to receive the cell or range of cells being copied.

To copy

1. Type /C.

2. The FROM: prompt requests the range of the cells to be copied. Highlight a range, or type the range name or the range address. Press **Enter**.

3. At the TO: prompt, specify the upper left corner of the range where you want the duplicate to appear by moving the cell pointer to that position. Press the period key (**.**) to anchor the first corner and press **Enter**.

Data Distribution

/DD

Purpose

Creates a frequency distribution showing how often specific data occur in a database.

Reminders

Works on only numeric values.

Data must be arranged in a column, row, or rectangular range. This is called the value range.

Move the cell pointer to a worksheet portion that has two adjacent blank columns. In the left column, enter the highest value for each entry in the bin range. Enter these bin values in ascending order.

To create a data distribution

1. Type **/DD**.

2. Enter the value range, which contains the data being analyzed, and then press **Enter**.

3. Enter the bin range, and then press **Enter**.

Note

The frequency distribution appears in the column to the right of the bin range. Note that the frequency column extends one row beyond the bin range.

Data Fill

/DF

Purpose

Fills a specified range with a series of equally incremented numbers, dates, times, or percentages.

Use **/Data Fill** to create date rows or columns, numeric rows or columns, headings for depreciation tables, sensitivity analyses, data tables, or databases.

Reminder

Numbers generated overwrite previous entries.

To fill a range

1. Type **/DF**.

2. Specify the range to be filled by highlighting the range, or by typing the address or range name, and then press **Enter**.

3. Enter the starting number, date, or time in the filled range and press **Enter**. The default value is 0.

4. When a Step value is requested, type the positive or negative number by which you want the value to be incremented and press **Enter**. The default value is 1. Date or time Step values require a numeric value followed by a letter to indicate the increment value.

   For dates, enter a value *n* followed by one of the following letters to indicate the increment unit:

   d to increment by *n* days

   w to increment by *n* weeks

   m to increment by *n* months

   q to increment by *n* quarters

   y to increment by *n* years

   For times, enter a value *n* followed by one of the following to indicate the increment unit:

   s to increment by *n* seconds

   min to increment by *n* minutes

   h to increment by *n* hours

   Date or time Step values can use special units. The default value is 1.

5. Enter a Stop value and press **Enter**.

Note

/Data Fill fills the range of cells column-by-column from top to bottom and from left to right until the Stop value is reached or the range is full.

Data Matrix Invert/Multiply

/DMI or /DMM

Purpose

Inverts columns and rows in square matrices. Multiplies column-and-row matrices of cells.

To invert a matrix

1. Type **/DM**.

2. Choose **I**nvert to invert a nonsingular square matrix of up to 90 rows and columns.

3. Specify the range you want to invert, and then press **Enter**.

4. Specify an output range or indicate the upper left corner of the output range to hold the inverted matrix. Press **Enter**.

To multiply matrices

1. Type **/DM**.

2. Choose **M**ultiply and highlight the two ranges to be multiplied. Press **Enter** after each range. The number of columns in the first range must be equal to the number of columns in the second range.

3. Indicate the upper left corner of the output range and press **Enter**.

Data Parse

/DP

Purpose

Separates the long labels resulting from **/F**ile **I**mport into distinct text and numeric cell entries. The separated text and numbers are placed in individual cells in a row of an output range.

To parse data

1. Move the cell pointer to the first cell in the row where you want to begin parsing.

2. Type **/DP**.

3. Select Format-Line.

4. Select Create. A format line is inserted at the cell pointer and the row of data moves down. This format line shows 1-2-3's "best guess" at how the data in the cell pointer should be separated.

5. You may need to change the format line to include or exclude data by selecting Edit from the Format-Line menu. Edit the format line and press **Enter**.

6. If the imported data is in different formats—an uneven number of items or a mixture of field names and numbers, for example—you must create additional format lines. Enter these lines at the row where the data format changed.

7. Select Input-Column.

8. Specify the column containing the format line and the data that you want to format.

9. Select Output-Range.

10. Move the cell pointer to the upper left corner of the range to receive the parsed data, and press **Enter**.

11. Select Go.

Data Query Criteria

/DQC

Purpose

Specifies the worksheet range containing the criteria that define which records you want to find.

Reminders

Indicate a criterion range before you use the Find, Extract, Unique, or Del options.

To specify the worksheet range of criteria

1. Type **/DQC**.

2. At the `Enter Criteria range:` prompt, specify or highlight the range that will contain field names and criteria. The range must contain at least two rows: the first row includes field names from the top row of the database you want to search, and the second row includes the criteria you specify.

Data Query Delete

/DQD

Purpose

Removes from the input range any records that meet conditions in the criterion range.

"Cleans up" your database by removing records that are not current or that you extracted to another worksheet.

Reminders

You must define a 1-2-3 database complete with input and criterion ranges.

Use /Data Query Find to ensure that your criteria is accurate before deleting those records that meet the specified conditions.

To remove records from the input range

1. Type **/DQD**.

2. Select **D**elete to remove the records from the input range or select **C**ancel or stop the command without deleting records.

3. Save the worksheet under a new file name using /**F**ile **S**ave. Using the same name will result in the original database being replaced with the database from which you deleted records.

Data Query Extract/Unique

/DQE or /DQU

Purpose

Copies to the output range of the worksheet records that meet conditions set in the criteria. /Data Query Unique copies only nonduplicate records and sorts them.

Reminder

You must define a 1-2-3 database complete with input, output, and criterion ranges before using /Data Query Extract or /Data Query Unique.

To copy the records meeting the criteria

1. Type **/DQE** to copy all records that meet the conditions set in the criteria.

   Or, type **/DQU** to copy nonduplicate records that meet conditions set in the criteria and to sort the copied records.

2. Select Quit to return to the worksheet.

Data Query Find

/DQF

Purpose

Finds records in the database that meet conditions you set in the criteria range.

Reminders

Works with only a single input range.

You must define the input range, external database (if one is used), and criteria range before using /Data Query Find.

To find records meeting conditions

1. Type **/DQF**.

   The cell pointer highlights the first record that meets the criteria. You will hear a beep if no record in the input range meets the criteria.

2. Press ↑ or ↓ to move to the next record that meets the criteria. Press **Home** or **End** to find the first or last record in the database that meets the criteria.

3. You can edit contents within a record. When the cell pointer highlights the cell you want to edit, press **F2** and edit the cell contents. Press **Enter**.

4. Return to the Data Query menu by pressing **Enter** or **Esc** when you are not in EDIT mode.

Data Query Input

/DQI

Purpose

Specifies a range of data records to be searched.

Reminders

You must indicate an input range before you use the **F**ind, **E**xtract, **U**nique, or **D**elete options.

The input range can be the entire database or a part of it and must include the field names. You can specify more than one data table.

To specify a range of records to be searched

1. Type **/DQI**.

2. At the `Enter input range:` prompt, specify the range of data records you want to search. Be sure to include in the range the field names at the top of the range and portions of the records that may be off the screen.

3. To specify more than one data table, use an argument separator—a comma (**,**), period (**.**), or semicolon (**;**)—to separate the input ranges. After you specify all the databases, press **Enter**.

Note

A defined input range is adjusted automatically if you insert or delete rows or columns within the range. The input line, however, must be redefined if you add or delete rows at the bottom or top of the input range.

Data Query Output

/DQO

Purpose

Assigns a location to which found records can be copied, by using the Extract or Unique commands.

Reminders

You must indicate an output range before you use the Extract and Unique options. The Find and Delete options do not use an output range.

To assign a location

1. Type **/DQO**.

2. At the prompt to enter the output range, specify the range to contain field names and the results of a search. Then press **Enter**.

Data Regression

/DR

Purpose

Finds trends in data and uses multiple-regression analysis to calculate the "best straight line" relating a single independent x value to a single dependent y value.

Reminder

The output area must be at least nine rows long, and must be two columns wider than the number of sets of x values (no less than four columns wide).

To calculate the "best straight line"

1. Type **/DR**.

2. Select **X**-Range, specify the range, which may contain up to 16 columns of independent variables, and press **Enter**. The values must be in adjacent columns.

3. Select **Y**-Range, specify the range containing a single column of dependent variables, and press **Enter**. This single column must have the same number of rows as the **X**-range.

4. Select **I**ntercept and choose **C**ompute (to calculate the Y-axis intercept automatically) or **Z**ero (to use zero as the Y-axis intercept).

5. Select **O**utput-Range and enter the cell address of the upper left corner of the output range.

6. Select **G**o to calculate the regression.

Data Sort

/DS

Purpose

Sorts the database in ascending or descending order.

Reminders

Sorting can be done on one or two fields (columns).

Do not include blank rows or the data labels at the top of the database when you highlight the data-range. Blank rows will sort to the top or bottom of the database, and the data labels will sort into the body of the database.

To sort data

1. Type **/DS** and select **D**ata-Range.

2. Highlight the data range to be sorted. You must include every field (column) in the database, but do not include the field labels at the top of the database, because this will cause the labels to be sorted with the data. Press **Enter**.

3. Select **P**rimary-Key, move the cell pointer to the column of the database that will be the primary key, and press **Enter**.

4. Specify **A**scending or **D**escending order and press **Enter**.

5. Select **S**econdary-Key if you want to sort duplicate copies of the primary key.

6. Specify Ascending or Descending order and press
    Enter.

7. Select Go.

Data Table 1/2

Purpose

Generates a table composed of one or two varying input
values and formulas. These commands are useful for
generating "what if" models.

Reminders

Use /Data Table 1 to show how changes in one variable
affect the output from one or more formulas. Use /Data
Table 2 to show how changes in two variables affect the
output from one formula.

To generate a table of input values and formulas

1. Type /DT1 or /DT2.

2. For /DT1, enter the table range so that it includes the
    Input 1 values or text in the extreme left column and
    the formulas in the top row.

    For /DT2, enter the table range so that it includes the
    Input 1 values in the extreme left column and the
    Input 2 values in the top row.

3. Enter the address for Input 1. For /DT2, enter the
    address for Input 2.

1-2-3 places the Input value(s) into the designated
cell(s), recalculates each formula, and places the results
in the data table.

File Admin Link-Refresh
/FAL

Purpose

Recalculates formulas in the current file that depend on data in other files.

Ensures that your worksheet is using current data when the files are shared between users (on a network, for example).

Reminder

Use /File Admin Link-Refresh before printing or reviewing final results if the current file is linked to other files that may have changed.

To recalculate formulas that depend on data in other files

Type **/FAL**.

File Admin Reservation
/FAR

Purpose

Controls the reservation status of a shared file on a network. A reservation is the ability to write to a file with the same file name.

To control a shared file's reservation status

1. Type **/FAR**.

2. Choose **G**et or **R**elease.

Note

If you do not have the file reservation, RO (for Read Only) appears at the bottom of the screen.

File Admin Table

/FAT

Purpose

Creates a table of files, which you select, on the worksheet. The table includes information about the file size, and the date and time the file was last modified.

Creates a list of files linked to the current file.

Reminder

Place the cell pointer in a blank area of the worksheet.

To create a table of files

1. Type **/FAT**.

2. Choose **W**orksheet, **P**rint, **G**raph, **O**ther, or **L**inked.

3. If you chose **W**orksheet, **G**raph, **P**rint, or **O**ther, press **Enter** to enter a table for the current directory. If you want a table from another directory, type the directory name and press **Enter**.

4. Highlight the range where you want to place the table and press **Enter**.

File Combine

/FC

Purpose

Combines values or formulas from a file or worksheet on disk into the current file.

Reminder

Copies the file on disk to the current file, adds values from the file on disk to the current file, and subtracts incoming values from the numeric values in the current file.

To combine values or formulas into the current file

1. Type **/FC**.

2. Select Copy, Add, or Subtract.

3. Select how much of the saved worksheet file you want to use.Choices include Entire-File or Named/Specified-Range.

4. If you select Named/Specified-Range, you are asked to enter the range name (or the range address) and the file name. If you select Entire-File, choose a file name. Press **Enter**.

File Directory

/FD

Purpose

Changes the current disk drive or directory for the current work session.

To change the current drive or directory

1. Type **/FD**.

2. If the displayed drive and directory are correct, press **Enter**. To change the settings, type a new drive letter and directory name and press **Enter**.

File Erase

/FE

Purpose

Erases 1-2-3 files from disk so that you have more available disk space.

Reminder

You cannot restore an erased file. Be sure that you will not need a file before you erase it.

To erase 1-2-3 files from disk

1. Type **/FE**.

2. Select the type of file you want to erase. Choices include Worksheet, Print, Graph, and Other.

3. Type the path and the name of the file, or use the
    arrow keys to highlight the file you want to erase.
    Press **Enter**.

4. Verify that you do or do not want to erase the file, by
    selecting **Y**es or **N**o from the menu.

File Import

/FI

Purpose

Brings ASCII text files into 1-2-3 worksheets.

Reminders

Remember that /File Import can be used in two ways to
transfer data into a 1-2-3 worksheet. The first method
reads each row of ASCII characters as left-aligned labels
in a column; the second method reads into separate cells
text enclosed in quotation marks or numbers surrounded
by spaces or separated by commas.

To import ASCII text

1. Move the cell pointer to the upper left corner of the
    range into which you want to import data.

2. Type **/FI**.

3. Choose how to import the ASCII file. Choices
    include **T**ext and **N**umbers.

4. Select the ASCII print file. Press **Enter**.

File List

/FL

Purpose

Displays all file names of a specific type that are stored
on the current drive and directory. Displays the size of
the file (in bytes) and the date and time the file was
created. In Rel. 2.2 and 2.3, lists the file referenced in
(linked to) formulas in the current file.

To display a file list

1. Type **/FL**.

2. Select the type of file you want to display. Choices include **W**orksheet, **P**rint, **G**raph, **O**ther, and **L**inked.

3. Use the arrow keys to highlight individual file names and to display specific information, such as the date and time a file was saved and its size in bytes.

4. Display files from a different directory by moving the cursor to a directory name and pressing **Enter**. Press **Backspace** to move to a parent directory.

5. Press **Enter** to return to the worksheet.

File Retrieve

Purpose

Loads the requested worksheet file from disk.

Reminders

The retrieved file replaces the current worksheet. Use /**F**ile **S**ave to store a current worksheet before you retrieve a new file.

To load a worksheet

1. Type **/FR**.

2. Select or type the file name you want to retrieve and press **Enter**.

Note

You can display a list of file names by pressing the F3 (Name) key in response to the prompt Name of file to retrieve.

File Save

Purpose

Saves the current worksheet and settings.

To save a file

1. Type **/FS**.

2. You can enter the file name for the worksheet by using the default name displayed; by using → or ← to highlight an existing name; by typing a new name; or by entering a new drive designation, path name, and file name. Press **Enter**.

3. If there is an existing file with the name you have selected, choose **B**ackup, **C**ancel, or **R**eplace.

Choosing **R**eplace replaces the existing file on disk with the worksheet you are saving. You cannot recover the replaced file. Use **B**ackup to save a copy of the original file.

To save a file with a password

1. Type **/FS**.

2. Type the file name, press the **space bar**, and type **P**. Press **Enter**.

3. Type a password of up to 15 characters (no spaces). A white square appears for each letter. Memorize the upper- and lowercase letter combination. You must enter the exact password. Press **Enter**.

4. At the verify prompt, type the password again and press **Enter**.

Note

You can change a protected file's password by using the **Backspace** key to delete the `Password Protected` message that appears when you use **/F**ile **S**ave. Then repeat steps 2 through 4.

File Xtract

Purpose

Saves to disk a portion of current worksheet as a separate worksheet.

Reminders

You can save the portion as it appears on the worksheet (with formulas) or save only the results of the formulas.

Extracted ranges that include formulas must include the cells to which the formulas refer, or the formulas will be incorrect.

If CALC appears at the bottom of the screen, calculate the file by pressing **F9** before extracting values.

To save part of the current worksheet

1. Position the cursor at the upper left corner of the range you want to extract.

2. Type **/FX**.

3. Choose **F**ormulas or **V**alues.

4. Type a file name other than the current worksheet name.

5. Specify the range of the worksheet to be extracted as a separate file. Press **Enter**.

6. If the file name already exists, choose **B**ackup, **C**ancel, or **R**eplace.

Graph/X/A/B/C/D/E/F

Purpose

Specifies the worksheet ranges containing x-axis and y-axis data or labels.

To specify a range for x-axis or y-axis data

1. Type /G.

2. Select the ranges for x- or y-axis data or labels to be entered from these options:

Menu Item	Function
X	Enters x-axis label range. These are labels such as *Jan*, *Feb*, *Mar*, and so on. Creates labels for pie graph wedges and line, bar, and stacked-bar graphs.
A	Enters first y-axis data range. The only data range used by a pie graph.
B	Enters second y-axis data range. Enters pie graph shading values and extraction codes.
C	Enters third y-axis data range. Enters pie graph control over display of percentage labels.
D-F	Enters fourth through sixth data ranges.

3. Indicate the data range by entering the range address, using a range name, or highlighting the range.

4. Press **Enter**.

Graph Group

/GG

Purpose

Quickly selects the data ranges for a graph, X and A through F, when data in adjacent rows and columns are in consecutive order.

To select graph data ranges
1. Type /GG.

2. Specify the range containing X and A through F data values. The rows or columns must be adjacent and in the order X, A, B, C, D, E, and F.

3. Select Columnwise if the data ranges are in columns or Rowwise if the data ranges are in rows.

Graph Name

/GN

Purpose
Stores graph settings for later use with the same worksheet.

Reminders
If you want to name a graph, make sure it is the active graph before naming it.

You can recall graphs in later work sessions only if you have saved the graph settings with /Graph Name Create, and then saved the worksheet with /File Save.

Be cautious when using the /Graph Name Reset command because it deletes all graph names in the current worksheet and all graph parameters.

To save graph settings
1. Type /GN.

2. Select one of the following options to name your file: Use, Create, Delete, Reset, or Table.

3. If you are switching to a new graph, creating a name, deleting, or resetting names, specify the name. If you are creating a table of graph names, specify the location for the graph.

Graph Options Color/B&W

/GOC or /GOB

Purpose

Defines the colors 1-2-3 uses to display graphs on your monitor.

To set the color option

Type **/GOC**.

To set the black and white option

Type **/GOB**.

Note

If you have a monochrome monitor, you should use **/GOB**, but if you print to a color printer, you must change to **/GOC**. If you have a color monitor and use **/GOC**, but you have a printer with only black-and-white capabilities, text will print in black and white.

Graph Options Data-Labels

/GOD

Purpose

Labels graph points from data contained in cells.

To label graph points

1. Type **/GOD**.

2. Select the data range to which you want to assign labels. Choices include **A-F**, **G**roup, and **Q**uit.

3. Specify the range containing the labels. This range should be the same size as the range you selected for A through F. If you are grouping data ranges, the range selected must be the same size as all the data ranges combined.

4. With Line or XY graphs, select the data label location relative to the corresponding data points from the following options: Center, Left, Above, Right, and Below.

5. Choose Quit, or return to Step 2 to enter more data labels.

Graph Options Format

/GOF

Purpose

Selects the symbols and lines that identify and connect data points.

Some line and XY graphs present information more clearly if the data is displayed only as data points; other graphs present information better if the data is represented by a series of data points linked with a solid line. Use /Graph Options Format to select the type of data points used for each data range (symbols, lines, or both).

To select formats for graph options

1. Type /GOF.

2. Select Graph to set the format for all ranges, or select A-F to define individually the data ranges to be formatted.

3. Select the data point type: Lines, Symbols, Both, Neither, and Area.

Graph Options Grid

/GOG

Purpose

Overlays a grid on a graph to enhance readability.

To use a graph grid

1. Type **/GOG**.

2. Select the type of grid. Choices include **H**orizontal, **V**ertical, **B**oth, and **C**lear.

Graph Options Legend

/GOL

Purpose

Indicates which line, bar, or point belongs to a specific y-axis data range.

Reminders

Y-axis data and legend titles for each range are entered in ranges A, B, C, D, E, and F. If, by using **/M**ove, **/W**orksheet **I**nsert, or **/W**orksheet **D**elete, you relocate a graph, 1-2-3 will not adjust cell addresses that have been used to create legends. To prevent this, use range names to describe legend ranges.

To specify a graph legend

1. Type **/GOL**.

2. Select **A**-**F** for individual ranges or **R**ange for all ranges.

3. If you chose **A** through **F**, enter the text for the legend. If you chose **R**ange, specify the range containing the legends.

Graph Options Scale

Purpose

Varies the scale along either x or y axes. The x-axis scale can be varied on XY-type graphs.

Reminders

Options within this command include the following:

- Making changes manually to the upper- or lower-axis end points.

- Choosing formats for numeric display. (Options are identical to those in /Worksheet Global Format or /Range Format.)

- Improving display of overlapping x-axis labels by skipping every specified occurrence, such as every second or third label.

To vary the axes scale

1. Type /GOS.

2. Select the axis or skip frequency to be changed. Choices include Y-Scale, X-Scale, and Skip.

3. If you select the Y-Scale or X-Scale menu items, select the menu item to be scaled. Choices include Automatic, Manual, Lower, Upper, Format, Indicator, Display, and Quit.

4. If you choose Skip, enter a number to indicate the frequency intervals at which the x-axis scale tick marks will appear. Press Enter.

Graph Options Titles

Purpose

Adds headings to the graph and to each axis.

To set graph headings

1. Type **/GOT**.

2. Select **F**irst, **S**econd, **X**-Axis, or **Y**-Axis to define the title to be entered.

3. Enter a title, cell address, or range name of a cell containing a title. Use cell contents for a title by entering a backslash (\ ) and the cell address or range name and pressing **Enter**.

Graph Reset

/GR

Purpose

Cancels all or some of a graph's settings so that you can create a new graph or exclude one or more data ranges from the old graph.

To cancel graph settings

1. Type **/GR**.

2. Choose **G**raph, **X**, **A-F**, **R**anges, **O**ptions, or **Q**uit.

Graph Save

/GS

Purpose

Saves the graph in a file with the extension .PIC to be used for printing graphs in PrintGraph, WYSIWYG, or other programs. Use **/G**raph **N**ame **C**reate and **/F**ile **S**ave to save the graph settings.

To save your graph

1. Type **/GS**.

2. Specify a file name and press **Enter**.

Graph Type

/GT

Purpose

Selects from among the 1-2-3 graph types. Each type of graph is best suited for displaying specific types of data.

To choose a graph type

1. Type /GT.

2. Select the type of graph:

Menu Item	Function
Line	Usually depicts a continuous series of data. Enter an X-axis label in the X range from the Graph menu.
Bar	Usually displays distinctly separate data series.
XY	Graphs data sets of x and y data; XY graphs have data on both axes.
Stack-Bar	Shows how proportions change within the whole.
Pie	Shows how the whole is divided into component portions. Use only the A range to contain the values of each portion. The X range is used to label the pie wedges.
HLCO	Tracks items that vary over time. Most commonly used in the stock market to show the price at which a stock opens and closes and its high and low price during the day.

Menu Item	Function
Mixed	Contains bar and line graphs. Relates trends in two distinct measurable quantities. If the scales for items vary significantly, a second Y axis (2Y Axis) can be added with a different scale. Mixed graphs can have up to three bars and three lines.
Features	Provides additional choices:

Vertical orients the graph vertically (default selection).

Horizontal rotates the graph so that the y-axis is horizontal and the x-axis is vertical.

Stacked stacks ranges on top of each other.

100% stacks ranges on top of each other as a percentage of the total. All stacks equal 100%.

Frame controls the adjustment of graph frame size, gutters, and zero lines.

Drop-Shadow enhances bar, stacked-bar, and mixed graphs by adding a three dimensional look.

| Quit | Returns to the Graph menu. |

3. The Graph menu reappears.

Graph View

/GV

Purpose

Displays a graph on-screen.

Reminders

Your system hardware and system configuration determine what is displayed on-screen.

To display a graph

1. Type /GV.

2. Press any key to return to the Graph menu.

3. Select Quit to return to READY mode.

Move

/M

Purpose

Moves ranges of labels, values, or formulas to different locations in the worksheet. Cell references and range names used in formulas stay the same, so formula results don't change.

To move data

1. Type /M.

2. The FROM: prompt requests the range of the cells to be moved. Highlight a range, or type the range name or the range address. Press Enter.

3. At the TO: prompt, enter the address of the single upper left corner of the range to which the cells will be moved. Press Enter.

Print Printer/File/Encoded /Background

/PP/F/E/B

Purpose

Prints worksheet contents and graphs.

/PP prints directly to the printer. /PF prints worksheet
contents as an ASCII text file to disk so that you may
import it into other programs. /PE prints a print-image
file to disk so that you can print it later. /PB sends print
output to an encoded file, and then prints it in the
background.

To print using these features

1. Type **/PP**, **/PF**, **/PE** or **/PB**.

2. For /PF or /PE, enter the print file name. With /PF,
    1-2-3 automatically gives the file name a .PRN
    extension. With /PE, 1-2-3 automatically gives the
    file name an .ENC extension. For /PB, specify the
    name of the encoded file.

3. Select **R**ange.

4. Specify the range or ranges to be printed.

5. Select other options as needed.

6. Select **G**o to print the range(s).

Print Printer Align

/PPA, /PFA, /PEA

Purpose

Aligns 1-2-3's internal line and page counter.

To set 1-2-3's page counter

1. If necessary, position the printer paper so that the top
    of a page is aligned with the printhead.

2. Type **/PP**, **/PF**, or **/PE**.

3. Select **A**lign to synchronize 1-2-3 with the printer.

Print Printer Clear

/PPC, /PFC, /PEC

Purpose

Clears print settings and options—the current print range and borders—and resets all formats (margins, page length, and setup strings) to default settings.

To reset print options to the defaults

1. Type **/PPC**, **/PFC**, or **/PEC**.

2. Select **A**ll, **R**ange, **B**orders, or **F**ormat.

Print Printer Line

/PPL, /PFL, /PEL

Purpose

Advances printer paper by one line.

To advance the paper by one line

1. Type **/PP**, **/PF**, or **/PE**.

2. Select **L**ine to advance the paper by one line. Repeat the keystroke (or press **Enter**) as many times as necessary to advance the paper to the location desired.

Note

The command /PFL puts a blank line in the PRN file.

Print Printer Options Borders

/PPOB, /PFOB, /PEOB

Purpose

Prints on every page the rows or columns selected from the worksheet.

Caution

If you include in the print range the rows or columns specified as borders, they will be printed twice.

To include the selected material on each printed page

1. Type /PPOB, /PFOB, or /PEOB.

2. Select Columns (to print specified columns at the left side of each page) or Rows (to print selected rows at the top of each page).

3. If necessary, press Esc to remove the current range. Specify the borders range. Press Enter.

Print Printer Options Footer/Header

/PPOF, /PPOH, /PFOF, /PFOH, /PEOF, /PEOH

Purpose

Prints a footer above the bottom margin or a header below the top margin of each page.

To print a header or footer

1. Type /PPO, /PFO, or /PEO.

2. Select Footer or Header.

3. You can type a footer or header as wide as the margin and paper widths allow. Press Enter.

Notes

Use headers and footers for titles, dates, and page numbers.

To print the date and page number automatically in the footer or header, enter an at sign (@) where you want the date to appear and a number sign (#) where you want the page number to appear.

Use \ followed by a cell address to insert the contents of a cell into the header or footer.

Separate the footer or header into as many as three centered segments by entering a split vertical bar (¦). To print in three segments with a system date of October 25, 1989, at page 21, for example, enter:

@ ¦ Hill and Dale ¦ Page #

This prints as:

25-Oct-89 Hill and Dale Page 21

To center the data, place one split vertical bar to the left of the data. To left-justify the data, do not include split vertical bars. To right-justify the data, insert two split vertical bars.

To right-justify the page number, for example, you enter:

¦ ¦ Page #

Print Printer Options Margins

/PPOM, /PFOM, /PEOM

Purpose

Changes the left, right, top, and bottom margins.

To set margins for printing

1. Type **/PPO**, **/PFO**, or **/PEO**.

2. Specify Margins. Choices include Left, Right, Top, Bottom, and None. The number you enter represents the number of characters.

Print Printer Options Other

/PPOO, /PFOO, /PEOO

Purpose

Prints the range as displayed (As-Displayed) or as a one-entry-per-line listing (Cell Formulas). You have options to print headers, footers, and page breaks (Formatted, Unformatted).

To use other print options

1. Type /PPOO, /PFOO, or /PEOO.

2. Select the printing method. Choices include As-Displayed, Cell-Formulas, Formatted, and Unformatted.

Print Printer Options Pg-Length

/PPOP, /PFOP, /PEOP

Purpose

Specifies the number of lines per page using a standard six-lines-per-inch page height.

To specify page length

1. Type /PPOP, /PFOP, or /PEOP.

2. Enter the number of lines per page if that number is different from the number shown. Page length can be from 1 to 100 lines. Press Enter.

Note

Four lines are used for top and bottom margins, and six lines are reserved for headers and footers. Therefore, the actual number of printable lines on a page is 56.

Print Printer Options Setup

/PPOS, /PFOS, /PEOS

Purpose

Sends commands to the printer for features not available
with 1-2-3 print commands.

Reminders

Your printer manual contains lists of printer setup codes
(also known as *printer control codes* or *escape codes*).

To choose printer setup codes

1. Type **/PPOS, /PFOS,** or **/PEOS**.

2. Enter the setup string. If a setup string has already
   been entered, press **Esc** to clear the string. Each
   control code must begin with a backslash (\) and
   must be typed as shown in your printer's manual.

3. Press **Enter**.

Note

Some codes start with the ESC character followed by
other characters. Because the ESC character cannot be
typed in the setup string, the ASCII decimal number for
ESC (27) is used instead. The EPSON printer code for
emphasized print, for example, is ESC "E". In the 1-2-3
setup string, enter ESC "E" as **\027E**.

Print Printer Page

/PPP, /PFP, /PEP

Purpose

Controls paper feed by moving the paper to the
bottom of the page for printing any footer, and then by
advancing the paper farther until the printhead is at the
top of the next page.

/PFP allows a footer and blank lines in a PRN file.

To position the paper for printing footers

1. Type **/PP**, **/PF**, or **/PE**.

2. Select **P**age to print any footer at the bottom of the page, and to position the printhead at the top of the next page.

Print Printer Range

/PPR, /PFR, /PER

Purpose

Defines the area of the worksheet to be printed.

To choose the area to be printed

1. Type **/PP**, **/PF**, or **/PE**. For /PF and /PE, specify a file name.

2. Select **R**ange.

3. Specify the range to be printed and press **Enter**.

4. Select any other necessary print options.

5. Select **G**o to print.

PrintGraph Commands

Purpose

PrintGraph commands print graphs saved from a worksheet with **/G**raph **S**ave. PrintGraph is a supplemental 1-2-3 utility available through the Lotus Access System menu or from the DOS prompt by typing **PGRAPH**.

PrintGraph Image Select

I

Purpose

Selects .PIC (graph) files to print or view. Use Image-Select to select multiple files you want printed in sequence.

Reminder

Use the worksheet to create and save a graph. After you save the graph and its settings to disk from the worksheet, the file name has a .PIC extension. Preview serves only as a reminder of which graph belongs to which file name. An on-screen graph does not look the same as the printed graph.

Use Settings Hardware Graphs-Directory to access the directory that contains the .PIC files.

To print or preview a graph

1. Select Image-Select from PrintGraph's menu to display a list of the current directory's .PIC files with their respective sizes and creation dates. A number sign (#) to the left of the file names marks previously selected graph files.

2. To mark a graph for printing, highlight the graph, and then press the space bar. Selected files are marked with #. Remove the markings by highlighting the graph file name and again pressing the space bar.

3. To preview the graph on-screen, highlight the file name and press F10 (Graph). Press any key to return to the Image-Select menu.

4. Press Enter to return to the PrintGraph menu. The graphs marked will print when you select Go.

5. The selected graph file names appear on the left side of PrintGraph's main screen. Graphs print in the order selected.

PrintGraph Go/Align/Page

G, A, P

Purpose

Activates the printing process, specifies the printhead position as the top of the page, and advances the paper one page at a time, respectively.

To use these commands

1. Check the status area of the PrintGraph screen to verify that the graphs selected have the correct image options, hardware setup, and action options necessary for the current printing.

2. Make sure that the printer has sufficient paper for the print job.

3. Position the printhead to the desired top-of-page position and make sure that the printer is on-line.

4. Select Go, Align, or Page.

PrintGraph Settings Action

SA

Purpose

Causes the printer to pause or stop between graphs.

To stop printing between graphs

1. Select Settings Action from the PrintGraph menu.

2. Select Pause Yes to pause the printer between graphs so that you can choose other print options or change the paper. Or select Eject Yes to print one graph per page by making the printer advance continuous-feed paper automatically to the next page after a graph prints.

Caution

Be sure to use Settings Action Pause Yes if your printer does not use continuous-feed paper or have an automatic sheet feeder.

Print Graph Settings Hardware

SH

Purpose

Defines for PrintGraph which directories contain graphs and fonts, determines the type(s) of printer(s) to use, how they connect to the PC, and specifies paper size.

To change the directory containing the font or graph files

1. Select Settings Hardware from PrintGraph's menu.

2. To change the directory, choose from these options:

Menu Item	*Function*
Graphs-Directory	Changes directory where .PIC files are located (for example, **C:\123\RESULTS**.
Fonts-Directory	Changes directory where font files are located (for example, **C:\123**).

To change your PC's interface (hardware connection) used to communicate to the printer or plotter:

1. Select Settings Hardware from PrintGraph.

2. Select Interface.

3. Select the interface that connects your printer or plotter to your PC from these options:

Setting	*Device*
1	First parallel printer (most printers)
2	First serial printer (most plotters)

Setting	Device
3	Second parallel printer
4	Second serial printer
5-8	DOS devices: LPT1: through LPT4:

4. If you selected a serial interface (options 2 or 4 in Step 3), enter the baud rate (transmission rate). You can find the recommended baud rate in your printer or plotter's manual.

Other options from the Settings Hardware menu include Printer (specifies the name of the graphics printer or plotter you are using) and Size-Paper (specifies the length and width of the paper).

PrintGraph Settings Image Font

SIF

Purpose

Determines the fonts (print styles) used for alphanumeric characters in a printed graph. With this command, you can use one font for the first line of the title and another for legends, other titles, and scale numbers.

To choose fonts

1. Make sure that the path to the Fonts Directory under HARDWARE SETTINGS is accurate. If it is not, select Settings Hardware Fonts-Directory to specify the directory in which the .FNT (Font) files are located. Press Enter and then Esc to return to the preceding menu selected by Settings.

2. Observe whether the default setting for font 1 and font 2 is BLOCK1. If you do not want to alter the default setting, proceed no further with this command. If you want to change one or both fonts, continue with the following steps.

3. Select Image Font.

4. Choose 1 to specify the print style for the top center
    title. Choose 2 to specify the print style for other titles
    and legends.

5. To choose a different font, use the ↑, ↓, Home, or
    End keys to point to the font you want.

6. Press the space bar to move the # marker to the
    desired font. Note that at this point the space bar is a
    toggle; pressing the space bar repeatedly turns the
    marker on and off.

7. Press Enter to select the font, or press Esc if you
    want 1-2-3 to ignore your action and to exit from the
    font menu.

8. Repeat Steps 4 through 7 if you want to select another
    font.

Note

Use Settings Save to make the PrintGraph Settings
specifications the default in the PGRAPH.CNF file.

Caution

You cannot choose print styles unless you correctly
specify the directory that stores the font instructions.

PrintGraph Settings Image Range-Colors

SIR

Purpose

Assigns available colors to specified graph ranges for
printing.

To assign colors

1. Select Settings from the PrintGraph menu.

2. If you have not designated a printer or plotter, select
    Hardware Printer. After you make your selection and
    press Esc, choose Image Range-Colors.

3. After you assign a color to one range, select another
    range and assign it a different color. Repeat this
    process until you assign a unique color to each range.

4. Select **Q**uit or press **Esc** to leave the **R**ange-Colors
    menu.

PrintGraph Settings Image Size

SIS

Purpose

Controls the location of the graph on the printed page,
including the graph's size and its rotation.

To choose the location of a graph on the page

1. At the PrintGraph menu, select **S**ettings **I**mage **S**ize.

2. Select the location/rotation of the graph(s) to be
    printed by choosing one of these menu options: **F**ull,
    Half, **M**anual. If you select Manual, you can set
    graph proportions, locations, and rotation with the
    following options: **T**op, **L**eft, **W**idth, **H**eight,
    Rotation.

Note

To print additional graphs on a single page, roll the
paper backward to align the paper's serrations with the
top of the printer's strike plate. Select *A*lign to reset the
top of the form. Use **S**ettings **I**mage **S**ize **M**anual to
adjust graph locations, sizes, and rotations so that graphs
do not overlap.

Quit

/Q

Purpose

Exits 1-2-3 and returns to the operating system.

Reminder

Files that are not saved with /File Save are lost when you exit 1-2-3.

To exit 1-2-3

1. Type /Q.

2. Select Yes to quit 1-2-3 and return to the operating system. Select No to return to the current worksheet.

3. If you do not save changes, another No/Yes menu appears. Select Yes to quit without saving your changes. Select No to return to the worksheet.

4. If you started 1-2-3 from the Access System menu, you will be returned to it. Choose Exit from the Access System menu to leave 1-2-3. If you started 1-2-3 by typing 123, you will be returned to the operating system.

Range Erase

/RE

Purpose

Erases the contents of a single cell or range of cells, but leaves the cell's format and protection status intact.

To erase a range

1. Type /RE.

2. Specify the range to be erased. Press Enter.

Range Format

/RF

Purpose

Prepares cells so that they are displayed with a specific format.

Reminders

Range formats take precedence over Worksheet Global formats.

/RF rounds only the appearance of the displayed number; it does not round the number used for calculation. As a result, displayed or printed numbers may appear to be incorrect answers to formulas. Use @**ROUND** to ensure that the values in calculations are rounded properly.

To format a range

1. Type **/RF**.

2. Select a format from the following menu items:

Menu Item	Function
Fixed	Sets the number of decimal places displayed.
Scientific	Displays large or small numbers, using scientific notation.
Currency	Displays currency symbols ($, for example) and commas.
,	Inserts commas to mark thousands and multiples of thousands.
General	Displays values with no special formatting.
+/−	Creates horizontal bar graphs or time-duration graphs on computers that do not have graphics capabilities. Each symbol is equal to one whole number. Positive numbers are displayed as plus (+) symbols; negative numbers are displayed as minus (−) symbols.

Menu Item	Function
Percent	Displays a decimal number as a whole percentage with a % sign.
Date	Displays serial-date numbers in the following formats. Select the corresponding number for formats.

1	DD-MMM-YY	12-Jan-89
2	DD-MMM	12-Jan
3	MMM-YY	Jan-89
4	MM/DD/YY	01/12/89
5	MM/DD	01/12

Menu Item	Function
Time	Displays time fractions.
Text	Evaluates formulas as numbers, but displays formulas as text on-screen.
Hidden	Hides contents from the display and does not print them, but still evaluates contents.
Reset	Returns the format to current /Worksheet Global format.

3. Enter the number of decimal places to be displayed if 1-2-3 prompts you to do so. The full value of a cell is used for calculation, not the value displayed.

4. Specify the range and press Enter.

Range Input

/RI

Purpose

Allows cell pointer movement in unprotected cells only.

Reminders

To use /Range Input effectively, organize your worksheet so that the data-entry cells are together.

Before you use /RI, use /Range Unprot to identify unprotected data entry cells. You do not have to enable /Worksheet Global Protection to use /RI.

To enable cell pointer movement in unprotected cells

1. Type /RI.

2. Specify the input range. Include a range that covers all cells in which you want to display or enter data.

3. Press Enter. The input range's upper left corner is moved to the screen's upper left corner. Cell-pointer movements are restricted to unprotected cells in the designated input range.

4. Make data entries using normal methods. Press Esc or Enter to exit /Range Input and return to normal cell pointer movement.

Range Justify

/RJ

Purpose

Fits text within a desired range by wrapping words to form complete paragraphs and redistributes words so that text lines are approximately the same length.

Note

/RJ justifies all contiguous text in a column until justification is stopped by nonlabel cell contents (a blank cell, a formula, or a value).

To justify text in a range

1. Type /RJ.

2. Highlight the range in which you want the text to be justified. If you do not specify a range, highlight only the first row of the text column.

3. Press Enter to justify the text. If you specified a range, worksheet cell contents in the extreme left

column of the highlighted range are justified; cells
outside the highlighted range do not move.

Range Label

Purpose

Selects how you want to align text labels in their cells.

To align labels

1. Type **/RL**.

2. Select **L**eft, **R**ight, or **C**enter.

3. Specify the range and press **Enter**.

Range Name

Purpose

Assigns a name to a cell or a range of cells.

Reminder

Pressing **F3**(Name) displays a list of names already in
use.

To create a range name

1. Type **/RN**.

2. Select **C**reate.

3. Type a range name consisting of up to 15 characters.
   Avoid using symbols other than the underline. Press
   Enter.

4. Specify the range to be named. Press **Enter**.

To create range names from labels

1. Type **/RN**.

2. Select **L**abels.

3. Select **R**ight, **D**own, **L**eft, or **U**p.

4. Specify the range of labels to be used as range names for adjacent cells. Press **Enter**.

To delete one or more range names

1. Type **/RN**.

2. Select **D**elete to delete a single range name. Select **R**eset to delete all range names.

3. If you select **D**elete, type or highlight the name you want to delete and press **Enter**. Formulas containing the range names will now use cell and range addresses.

To create a table of existing range names and addresses

1. Move the cell pointer to a clear area of the worksheet.

2. Type **/RN**.

3. Select **T**able. Press **Enter**.

Notes

Instead of cell addresses, use range names to make formulas and macros easy to read and understand.

Use a range name when you enter a function. Instead of entering a function as **@SUM(P53..P65)**, for example, you could type it as **@SUM(EXPENSES)**.

Use a range name when you respond to a prompt. When the program requests a print range, for example, provide a range name, as in the following example:

```
Enter print range: JULREPORT
```

Range Prot/Unprot

/RP, /RU

Purpose

Changes the protection status of a range.

Use **/RP**, **/RU**, and **/W**orksheet **G**lobal **P**rotection to protect worksheets from accidental changes. **/RU**

identifies which cell contents can be changed when
/**W**orksheet **G**lobal **P**rotection is enabled.

To unprotect a cell or a range of cells

1. Type /**RU**.

2. Specify the range and press **Enter**.

To remove the unprotected status from a range

1. Type /**RP**.

2. Specify the range to be unprotected and press **Enter**.

Note

The contents of unprotected cells increase in intensity or
change color, depending on your graphics hardware.

Range Search
/RS

Purpose

Locates and replaces one string (in a label, formula, or
both) with another.

Reminders

You cannot use /**RS** to find or replace numbers, unless
the numbers are part of a label or formula.

To search and replace text

1. Type /**RS**.

2. Specify the range you want to search.

3. Enter the text string you want to find or replace.
   Either upper- or lowercase text may be used.

4. Choose **F**ormulas, **L**abels, or **B**oth.

5. Choose **F**ind or **R**eplace.

6. If you choose **F**ind, 1-2-3 will find and display the
   cell that contains the first occurrence of the specified
   text. Choose **N**ext to find other occurrences, or
   choose **Q**uit to stop the search.

If you choose Replace, type the replacement string and press Enter. 1-2-3 finds and displays the cell that contains the first occurrence of the specified text. You can then choose Replace, All, Next, or Quit.

7. After all occurrences are found, press Esc or Enter to return to READY mode.

Range Trans

/RT

Purpose

Reorders columns of data into rows, or rows of data into columns.

Reminder

Transpose the new data to a clear worksheet area. The transposed data overwrites any existing data.

To transpose data from rows to columns or columns to rows

1. Type /RT.

2. Specify the range to be transposed. Press Enter.

3. When 1-2-3 displays the TO: prompt, move the cell pointer to the upper left of the destination cells and press Enter.

Range Value

/RV

Purpose

Replaces formulas in the same or new location with their resulting values.

To replace formulas with values

1. Type /RV.

2. Specify the source range. Press Enter.

3. Specify the upper left corner cell of the destination range.

4. Press Enter. The values appear in the destination range. These values preserve the numeric formats used in the original formulas.

System

/S

Purpose

Exits 1-2-3 temporarily so that you can run DOS commands or other programs, and returns to 1-2-3 and the current worksheet.

Reminder

Be certain that the programs you run from 1-2-3 will fit in your computer's available memory. It is best not to load or run memory-resident programs while in System.

To exit to DOS

1. Type /S.

2. Type the DOS commands or programs you want to execute.

3. When you finish running a program, return to DOS.

4. To return to 1-2-3 from the DOS prompt, type EXIT and press Enter.

Worksheet Column

/WC

Purpose

Adjusts or hides the column width of one or more columns.

To set a new column width or hide a column

1. Type /WC.

2. Select Set-Width, Reset-Width, Hide, Display, or Column-Range.

3. If you chose Set-Width, enter the new column width by typing the number of characters, or by pressing ← or → to shrink or expand the column. To reset the column width to the default, select Reset-Width.

   If you chose Hide, indicate which columns you want to change. To display hidden columns (which have an asterisk beside the column letter), highlight the columns you want to redisplay.

   If you chose Column-Range, choose Set-Width, indicate the columns you want to change, and enter the column width as a number, or you can press ← or → to shrink or expand the column.

   To reset column widths to the default, select Reset-Width and highlight the columns you want to change.

4. Press Enter.

Worksheet Delete

/WD

Purpose

Deletes one or more columns or rows from the worksheet.

Procedures

1. Type /WD.

2. Select Column or Row.

3. Specify a range containing the columns or rows you want to delete.

4. Press Enter.

Worksheet Erase

/WE

Purpose

Erases the entire worksheet and resets all cell formats, label prefixes, and command settings to their original values so that you have a fresh work area.

Reminder

Be sure to save the current worksheet before you use /Worksheet Erase.

To erase the worksheet

1. Type /WE.

2. Select Yes or No.

3. If you haven't saved the latest changes, 1-2-3 warns you by beeping and displaying another Yes/No menu. Choose No to cancel the command or Yes to erase without saving.

Worksheet Global Column-Width

/WGC

Purpose

Sets column width for the entire worksheet.

To set the worksheet column width

1. Type /WGC.

2. Enter a number for the column width used most frequently, or press → to increase column width or ← to decrease column width.

3. Press Enter.

Worksheet Global Default

/WGD

Purpose

Specifies display formats and start-up settings for hardware.

Used to control how 1-2-3 works with the printer, which disk and directory are accessed automatically, which international displays are used, and whether the clock or file name is displayed.

To specify 1-2-3 defaults

1. Type /WGD.

2. Select the setting you want to change:

Menu Item	Function
Printer	Specifies printer settings and connections. Choose from the following options:

Interface selects parallel or serial port.

AutoLF instructs 1-2-3 to insert a line feed automatically after each printer line.

Left Margin (Choose from 0 to 240; the default is 4).

Right Margin (Choose from 0 to 240; the default is 76).

Top Margin (Choose from 0 to 32; the default is 2).

Bot Margin (bottom margin) (Choose from 0 to 32; the default is 2).

Pg-Length (Choose from 1 to 100; the default is 66).

Menu Item	*Function*
	Wait pauses for page insert at the end of each page.
	Setup sets the initial printer-control codes.
	Name selects from multiple printers.
	Delay specifies the number of minutes to wait before generating printer error.
	Quit returns to the Printer menu.
Directory	Specifies the directory for read or write operations. Press **Esc** to clear. Type the new directory and press **Enter**.
Status	Displays settings for /**W**orksheet **G**lobal **D**efault.
Update	Saves to disk the current global defaults for use with the next startup.
Other	Enables you to choose from the following options:
	International specifies display settings for **P**unctuation, **C**urrency, **D**ate, **T**ime, and **N**egative formats.
	Help enables you to choose whether the Help file is immediately accessible from disk (Instant) or whether it can be removed (Removable).
	Clock displays **S**tandard or **I**nternational date and time formats or **N**one. **C**lock displays date and time indicator, and **F**ilename displays current file name.

Menu Item	Function
	Undo enables or disables the undo feature. When enabled, allows you to cancel an operation immediately after you execute it. You can use Alt-F4 (Undo).
	Beep turns the computer's error sound on or off.
	Add-in lets you specify an add-in application to be attached automatically, each time you load 1-2-3. You also can designate the number of the function key (7 to 10) to invoke the add-in.
	Expanded Memory controls how 1-2-3 uses expanded memory. Standard maximizes the speed (initial default); Enhanced allows large worksheets.
Autoexec	Enables or disables the capability to automatically run autoexecute macros when files are retrieved.
Quit	Returns you to the worksheet.

Worksheet Global Format

/WGF

Purpose

Defines the default display format for numeric values and formulas in the entire worksheet, except those cells already formatted with /Range Format.

Procedures

1. Type /**WGF**.

2. Select one of the following formats: **F**ixed, **S**cientific, **C**urrency, **,** (comma), **G**eneral, +/−, **P**ercent, **D**ate, **T**ext, or **H**idden. (See *Range Format* for a detailed explanation of these commands.)

3. After you select **F**ixed, **S**cientific, **C**urrency, **,** (comma), or **P**ercent, enter the number of decimal places. Press **Enter**. Numbers that are stored in the cells are accurate up to 15 digits to the right of the decimal. The stored numbers, not the displayed numbers, are used in calculations.

Worksheet Global Label-Prefix

/WGL

Purpose

Selects text label alignment throughout the worksheet.

To align label text

1. Type /**WGL**.

2. Select **L**eft, **R**ight, or **C**enter.

3. Type the labels as you want them to appear on the worksheet.

Worksheet Global Protection

/WGP

Purpose

Protects the entire worksheet from being changed or removes existing protection.

Reminder

Before or after you protect the entire worksheet, you can
use **/R**ange **U**nprot to specify cells that can be modified.

To protect your worksheet

1. Type **/WGP**.

2. Select **E**nable to protect the worksheet so that only
   cells specified with **/R**ange **U**nprot can be changed.

   Select **D**isable to remove protection from the
   worksheet so that any cell can be changed.

Worksheet Global Recalc

/WGR

Purpose

Defines how files recalculate and how many times they
calculate.

To set worksheet recalculation

1. Type **/WGR**.

2. Select one of the following:

Menu Item	Function
Natural	Calculates formulas in the order the results are needed.
Columnwise	Starts at the top of column A and recalculates downward, then moves to column B, recalculating downward, and so on.
Rowwise	Starts at the beginning of row 1 and recalculates to the end, then continues through following rows.
Automatic	Recalculates when cell contents change.

Menu Item	Function
Manual	Recalculates only when you press the F9 (Calc) key or when {CALC} is encountered in a macro. The CALC indicator appears at the bottom of the screen when recalculation is advised.
Iteration	Recalculates the worksheet a specified number of times.

3. If you select Iteration, enter a number from 1 to 50. The default setting is 1. Iteration works with Columnwise and Rowwise recalculations or with Natural recalculation when the worksheet contains a circular reference.

4. If you select Columnwise or Rowwise recalculation, you may need to repeat Step 1 and select Iteration in Step 2. In Step 3, enter the number of recalculations necessary for correct results. Columnwise and Rowwise recalculations often require multiple calculations to ensure that all worksheet results are correct.

Worksheet Global Zero

/WGZ

Purpose

Suppresses zeros from appearing in displays and printed reports, or displays a label instead.

To suppress zero display

1. Type /WGZ.

2. Choose from the following commands:

Menu Item	Function
No	Displays cells containing zero or a result of zero as zero.
Yes	Suppresses the display of cells containing zero or a result of zero; zero values are displayed as blank cells.
Label	Displays a label that you enter in place of zero values.

3. If you choose Label, enter the label you want to display and press Enter. Precede the label with an apostrophe (') for left alignment, double quotation mark (") for right alignment, or caret (^) for centered text. The default label alignment is set at right alignment.

Worksheet Insert

/WI

Purpose

Inserts one or more blank columns or rows in the worksheet.

To insert a row or column into your worksheet

1. Type /WI.

2. Select Column or Row.

3. Highlight one cell for each column or row you want to insert.

4. Press Enter.

Worksheet Learn

/WL

Purpose

Specifies a worksheet range to record keystrokes when you type them.

Recording your keystrokes saves you from having to write down or memorize the keystrokes for your macros.

Reminder

Use /Worksheet Learn Range command to specify a learn range to store keystrokes in the worksheet.

To specify a range for recording keystrokes

1. Position the cell pointer at the top of the column in which you want to store keystrokes.

2. Type /WLR.

3. Highlight a single column and press Enter.

4. To begin recording keystrokes, press Alt-F5 (Learn). Enter all keystrokes, and press Alt-F5 to turn off the recording.

5. Go to the learn range and edit the macro keystrokes if necessary.

6. Name the macro with /Range Name Create.

To clear or cancel a learn range

1. Type /WL.

2. Select Cancel to cancel an existing learn range without erasing any keystrokes in the learn range, or choose Erase to clear all the keystrokes presently recorded in the learn range.

Notes

Make certain that you define a LEARN range which is large enough to accommodate your macro instructions. If you do not, 1-2-3 turns off the LEARN range when the defined area is filled.

Some special keys and mouse actions are not recorded
by 1-2-3 in the learn range. LEARN will record HELP
(F1), but will not record any keystrokes entered while
using HELP.

Worksheet Page

/WP

Purpose

Manually inserts page breaks in printed worksheets.

Reminder

Before you use /Worksheet Page, move the cellpointer
to the leftmost column of the range and one row below
the line you want the page break in.

To insert a page break

1. Type /WP.

2. A row is inserted and a double colon (::) appears in
   the left column.

   Use /Worksheet Delete Row or /Range Erase to
   remove the page break.

Worksheet Status

/WS

Purpose

Displays the current global settings and hardware
options. Also checks available memory.

To check your worksheet's status

1. Type /WS.

2. Press any key to return to the worksheet.

Worksheet Titles

/WT

Purpose

Displays row or column headings that might otherwise be scrolled off the screen.

Reminders

If you want column headings at the top of the screen, move the cell pointer so that the column headings you want to freeze on-screen occupy the top rows of the spreadsheet.

If you want row headings along the extreme left edge of the screen, move the cell pointer so that the column containing the extreme left-row headings are at the left edge of the screen.

Move the cell pointer one row below the lowest row to be used as a title, and one column to the right of the column(s) to be used as a title(s).

To keep headings on-screen

1. Type /WT.

2. Select Both, Horizontal, Vertical, or Clear.

Worksheet Window

/WW

Purpose

Displays two parts of the worksheet at the same time.

You can split the worksheet horizontally or vertically. The two parts of the worksheet can scroll separately or together, following the same cell pointer movements.

To use a worksheet window

1. Type /WW.

2. Select one of the following menu items:

Menu Item	*Function*
Horizontal	Splits the worksheet into two horizontal windows at the cell pointer.
Vertical	Splits the worksheet into two vertical windows at the cell pointer.
Sync	Synchronizes two windows so that they scroll together. Sync is the default setting.
Unsync	Enables you to scroll two windows independently of each other.
Clear	Removes the right or bottom window.

1-2-3 FUNCTIONS

For an in-depth discussion of 1-2-3 functions, see Que's *Using 1-2-3 Release 2.3*. For the functions that take an *attribute* (the information returned about a cell), refer to the following list:

Attribute	*Cell Information Returned*
"address"	Cell address (column and row)
"col"	Cell column (1 to 256)
"contents"	Cell contents
"filename"	Name of file
"format"	Format code
"prefix"	Label prefix
"protect"	1 if protected, 0 if not protected
"row"	Cell row number (1 to 8,192)
"type"	b for blank, v for value, l for label
"width"	Column width

This section provides all 1-2-3 functions in alphabetical order:

@@(*cell address*)

@?

@ABS(*x*)

@ACOS(*x*)

@ASIN(*x*)

@ATAN(*x*)

@ATAN2(*x,y*)

@AVG(*range*)

@CELL(*attribute,range*)

@CELLPOINTER(*attribute*)

@CHAR(*x*)

@CHOOSE(*key,v1,v2,v3, ...vn*)

@CLEAN(*string*)

@CODE(*string*)

@COLS(*range*)

@COS(*x*)

@COUNT(*range*)

@CTERM(*int, fv,pv*)

@DATE(*yy,mm,dd*)

@DATEVALUE(*date string*)

@DAVG(*input range, field,criterion range*)

@DAY(*date number*)

@DCOUNT(*input range, field,criterion range*)

@DDB(*cost,salvage,life,period*)

@DMAX(*input range, field,criterion range*)

@DMIN(*input range, field, criterion range*)

@DSTD(*input range, field,criterion range*)

@DSUM(*input range, field,criterion range*)

@DVAR(*input range,field,criterion range*)

@ERR

@EXACT(*string1,string2*)

@EXP(*x*)

@FALSE

@FIND(*search string,target string,start number*)

@FV(*pmt,int,term*)

@HLOOKUP(*test,range,row offset number*)

@HOUR(*time number*)

@IF(*test condition,true result,false result*)

@INDEX(*range,column,row*)

@INT(*x*)

@IRR(*int guess,range*)

@ISAAF

@ISAPP

@ISERR

@ISNA(*x*)

@ISNUMBER(*x*)

@ISSTRING(*x*)

@LEFT(*string,n*)

@LENGTH(*string*)

@LN(*x*)

@LOG(*x*)

@LOWER(*string*)

@MAX(*range*)

@MID(*string,start number,n*)

@MIN(*range*)

@MINUTE(*time number*)

@MOD(*x,y*)

@MONTH(*date number*)

@N(*range*)

@NA

@NOW

@NPV(*int,range*)

@PI

@PMT(*principal,int,term*)

@PROPER(*string*)

@PV(*pmt,int,term*)

@RAND

@RATE(*fv,pv,term*)

@REPEAT(*string,n*)

@REPLACE(*original string,start number,length, new string*)

@RIGHT(*string,n*)

@ROUND(*x,n*)

@ROWS(*range*)

@S(*range*)

@SECOND(*time number*)

@SIN(*x*)

@SLN(*cost,salvage,life*)

@SQRT(*x*)

@STD(*range*)

@STRING(*x,n*)

@SUM(*range*)

@SYD(*cost,salvage,life,period*)

@TAN(*x*)

@TERM(*pmt,int,fv*)

@TIME(*hr,min,sec*)

@TIMEVALUE(*time string*)

@TRIM(*string*)

@TRUE

@UPPER(*string*)

@VALUE(*string*)

@VAR(*range*)

@VLOOKUP(*test,range,column offset number*)

@YEAR(*date number*)

1-2-3 MACROS

Macros are text labels that automate the same keystrokes you enter when using 1-2-3. The macro to widen a column's width to 12 characters, for example, is

'/wcs12~

The apostrophe tells 1-2-3 that the following characters are text. If you do not enter an apostrophe first, 1-2-3 will not recognize that you are entering a macro and will display the main menu when you press the slash key.

The characters that follow the introductory apostrophe represent the keystrokes used to widen a column's width: /Worksheet Column Set-Width 12.

The tilde (~) in a macro represents pressing **Enter**.

You type macros in three columns located below the worksheet's calculation area: one column for the macro's name (a reminder to the user), one column for the macro code, and one column to explain the macro code.

To create and test a macro

1. Move the cell pointer to an area below and to the right of the worksheet's calculation area. Placing the macro away from the calculation area ensures that you will not accidentally interfere with the macro as you work.

2. Enter the macro's title (for example, **DATE ENTRY**) as a reminder of the macro's function.

3. Move the cell pointer down one cell and one cell to the left. Enter the macro's name (an apostrophe, followed by a backslash, followed by a single letter or the number zero). For example, '\C.

4. Move the cell pointer to the right one cell. Enter the first cell of macro code (keystrokes). Enter a single process or task into each cell.

5. Move the cell pointer to the third column, adjacent to the code. Enter a brief explanation that will help you and others remember how the macro works.

6. Move the cell pointer below the first cell of macro code and enter the next cell of macro code. Continue entering code and explanations. Do not leave a blank cell in the macro-code column, because this will stop the macro.

7. Move the cell pointer to the first cell of macro code.

8. Use **/R**ange **N**ame **C**reate to give the first cell of code a range name.

9. Use **/F**ile **S**ave to save your worksheet with a temporary name.

10. Make backup copies of the worksheet, including the macro and any files involved with the macro.

11. Test the macro by moving the cell pointer to a location appropriate for the macro. Invoke the macro by holding down the **Alt** key and quickly pressing the letter in the macro name (for example, **Alt-C**) or press **Alt-F3** (Run) and type or select the macro name.

The STEP Mode

Purpose

Troubleshoots macros. Checks a macro for errors before you run the macro.

Use 1-2-3's STEP mode to view the macro as it executes one code character at a time. With STEP, you can see where the error is located in the macro.

To use STEP mode

1. Print a copy of your macro on paper.

2. Press the STEP key (**Alt-F2**).

3. Start the macro by holding down the **Alt** key and pressing the letter you have assigned to the macro or press **Alt-F3** (Run) and type or select the macro name.

   The mode indicator will display READY, and SST will flash at the bottom of the screen.

4. Press the **space bar** slowly. With each press, the macro executes one character or macro command. 1-2-3 beeps if the macro encounters an incorrect or out-of-sequence command.

5. To exit the macro, press **Ctrl-Break**. You may have to press **Esc** after exiting the macro.

6. Based on the macro's execution in STEP mode, check the macro code at the location where you think an error has occurred. Use EDIT mode (**F2**) to make corrections.

7. STEP mode remains activated until you press **Alt-F2** again.

Macro Commands

The following is a list of commands that you can use in your macros. For an in-depth discussion of macro commands, see Que's *Using 1-2-3 Release 2.3*.

{APPENDBELOW *source,destination*}

{APPENDRIGHT *source,destination*}

{BEEP *number*} or {BEEP}

{BLANK *location*}

{BORDERSOFF}

{BORDERSON}

{BRANCH *location*}

{BREAK}

{BREAKOFF}

{BREAKON}

{CLOSE}

{CONTENTS *destination,source,width,format*}

{DEFINE *loc1:Type1,...*}

{DISPATCH *location*}

{FILESIZE *location*}

{FOR *counter,start,stop,step,routine*}

{FORBREAK}

{FORM *input,call-table,include-keys,exclude-keys*}

{FORMBREAK}

{FRAMEOFF}

{FRAMEON}

{GET *location*}

{GETLABEL *prompt,location*}

{GETNUMBER *prompt,location*}

{GETPOS *location*}

{GRAPHOFF}

{GRAPHON *named-graph,no-display*}

{IF *condition*}{*true*}

{INDICATE *string*}

{LET *location,expression*}

{LOOK *location*}

{MENUBRANCH *location*}

{MENUCALL *location*}

{ONERROR *branch,message*}

{OPEN]

{PANELOFF}

{PANELON}

{PUT *range,col,row,value*}

{QUIT}

{READ *bytecount,location*}

{READLN *location*}

{RECALC *location,condition,iteration-number*}

{RECALCCOL *location,condition,iteration-number*}

{RESTART}

{RETURN}

{SETPOS *file-position*}

{SUBROUTINE}

{SYSTEM *command*}

{WAIT *argument*}

{WINDOWSOFF}

{WINDOWSON}

{WRITE *string*}

{WRITELN *string*}

Macro Key Codes

The keystroke instructions automate single-key activities (for example, Home, End, or Esc), within macros. Using **{HOME}** in a macro, for example, moves the cell pointer to the upper left corner of the active window.

Use the following macro instructions to perform certain key functions.

Instruction	Keyboard Key
{?}	(waits for user input)
~	Enter
{ABS}	F4 (Abs)
{APP1}	Alt-F7 (App1)

{APP2}	Alt-F8 (App2)
{APP3}	Alt-F9 (App3)
{APP4}	Alt-F10 (Addin)
{BS}	Backspace
{BIGLEFT}	Tab
{BIGRIGHT}	Shift-Tab
{CALC}	F9 (Calc)
{DEL}	Del
{DOWN} or {D}	Down-arrow key ($\downarrow$)
{EDIT}	F2 (Edit)
{END}	End
{ESC}	Esc
{GOTO}	F5 (GoTo)
{GRAPH}	F10 (Graph)
{HELP}	F1(Help)
{HOME}	HOME
{INSERT} or {INS}	Insert
{LEFT}	Left-arrow key($\leftarrow$)
{MENU}	(Initiates the command menu)
{NAME}	F3 (Name)
{PGDN}	PgDn
{PGUP}	PgUp
{QUERY}	F7 (Query)
{RIGHT}	Right-arrow key ($\rightarrow$)
{TABLE}	F8 (Table)
{UP}	Up-arrow key ($\uparrow$)
{WINDOW}	F6 (Window)
{{}	Open brace
{}}	Close brace

VIEWER

Purpose

Viewer is 1-2-3's add-in program that enables you to
retrieve, link or browse through the contents of a 1-2-3
file or the text of any other type of file on your hard
disk.

Viewer also displays the DOS directory information and
makes it easier to enter procedures for linking formulas.

Reminder

Data is displayed on a split screen where the file names
of your current directory are displayed on the left in the
List window and their contents are displayed on the right
in the View window.

Viewer must be attached with /Add-in Attach before it
can be invoked.

To view the contents of the file you selected from the
List window, press → to move to the View window (or
click the left mouse button in the View window).

To use Viewer

1. Choose /Addin Invoke Viewer

2. Select the function you want to perform from the
   following menu items:

Menu Item	Function
Browse	Enables you to view the contents of a list of files in the current directory displayed in the List window without retrieving them.
Link	Allows the linking of the current cell or range to a cell or range you select from another worksheet, which can be any of the files listed in the List window (.WK1, .WKS, .WR1, and .WRK worksheet files in the current directory). Link formulas are created when the cell pointer resides in the target cell, the Viewer is invoked,

the source range is identified, the
pointer is placed in the source cell,
and **Enter** is pressed.

Retrieve   Allows you to scroll through a list of
worksheet files displayed in the
View window, which enables you to
view their contents and select the
file you want to retrieve.

USING WYSIWYG

1-2-3 Release 2.3 provides you with the tools you need
to present your spreadsheets in an attractive format by
including the WYSIWYG spreadsheet publishing
add-in.

WYSIWYG commands enable you to add and edit
worksheet graphics, format data, print presentation-
quality documents, and customize the way 1-2-3
displays worksheets on-screen.

This section provides an alphabetical listing of all
the WYSIWYG commands. Before you can use
WYSIWYG commands, you must attach the program.

To load the program into memory

1. Press **Alt-F10** (ADDIN).

2. Press **A**.

3. Select WYSIWYG.ADN and press **Enter**.

4. If you do not want to assign a function key to
   WYSIWYG, press **N**.

   To assign a function key, press **7**, **8**, **9**, or **10**. These
   numbers correspond to function keys **Alt-F7**, **Alt-F8**,
   Alt-F9, and **Alt-10**.

5. Press **Q**.

Note

Once WYSIWYG is attached, in order to invoke it,
1-2-3 must be in READY mode. You can either press

colon (:) or click the right mouse button anywhere in the
control panel, to switch between the 1-2-3 and
WYSIWYG menus.

Display Colors

:DC

Purpose

Specifies worksheet colors for background, text, cell
pointer, grid, worksheet frame, lines, drop shadows,
negative values, and data in unprotected ranges. Also
modifies the hue of the eight colors that 1-2-3 uses with
WYSIWYG.

Note

For all the Display commands: to update WYSIWYG so
that it uses the new color settings in future sessions,
select :Display Default Update.

Reminder

WYSIWYG must be in graphics display mode (:Display
Mode Color).

Display Colors is the only Display command that affects
worksheets or graphics you print; it affects worksheets
and graphics only if you have a color printer.

To display color

1. Type :DC.

2. Select one of the following commands. For each
   command you can choose from Black, White, Red,
   Green, Dark Blue, Cyan, Yellow, and Magenta.

Menu Item	Function
Background	Determines the color of the worksheet background. Choose a color.

Text   Determines the color for worksheet
                text. Choose a color.

Unprot   Determines the color for data in
                ranges where global protection has
                been removed with the **/R**ange
                Unprot command. Choose a color.

Cell-Pointer   Determines the color for the cell
                pointer. Choose a color.

Grid   Determines the color for the
                worksheet grid lines set with the
                :Display **O**ptions **G**rid **Y**es
                command. Choose a color.

Frame   Determines the color for the
                worksheet frame. Choose a color.

Neg   Determines the default color of
                negative values. Choose a color.

Lines   Determines the color of cell borders
                added to the worksheet with the
                :Format **L**ines command. Choose a
                color.

Shadow   Determines the color for drop
                shadows added to the worksheet
                with the **:F**ormat **L**ines **S**hadow **S**et
                command. Choose a color.

Replace   Modifies the hue of the eight
                WYSIWYG colors. Select a number
                from **0** to **63**.

Display Default

:DD

Purpose

Creates a new set of default display settings or replaces current display settings with default display settings.

Reminder

The default display settings are stored in the WYSIWYG configuration file, WYSIWYG.CNF. 1-2-3 uses this file automatically whenever you attach the WYSIWYG add-in.

To change the default settings

1. Type :DD.

2. Select from these menu items:

Menu Item	Function
Restore	Replaces the current display settings with the default display settings.
Update	Saves the current display settings as the default display settings.

Display Font-Directory

:DF

Purpose

Specifies the directory where 1-2-3 looks for the fonts that it needs for the screen display and for printing.

Reminder

If you select a directory without font files, 1-2-3 displays and prints in the system font, which is Courier.

To specify the font directory

1. Type :**DF**.

2. Press **Esc** to delete the current directory setting.

3. Type the drive letter and path name of the new directory.

Note

The default font directory is the WYSIWYG subdirectory of the 1-2-3 Release 2.3 program directory; for example,

C:\123R23\WYSIWYG>

Display Mode

:DM

Purpose

Changes between graphics and text display modes, and between black-and-white and color.

Reminder

Graphics display mode is the WYSIWYG default mode. Color and black-and-white work in only graphics display mode.

To change the display mode

1. Type :**DM**.

2. Select one of the following choices:

Menu Item	*Function*
Graphics	Sets the worksheet display to look like the final printed output.
Text	Sets the worksheet display to look like standard 1-2-3 without WYSIWYG.

Menu Item	Function
B&W	Sets worksheet display to black-and-white (monochrome).
Color	Sets worksheet display to color.

Note

In graphics display mode, the screen display looks like your final printed output.

Display Options

:DO

Purpose

Affects the display of grid lines, page breaks, worksheet frame, and the cell pointer. Also affects brightness.

To change the display options

1. Type **:DO**.

2. Select one of the following choices:

Menu Item	Function
Frame	Changes the appearance or hides the 1-2-3 worksheet frame. Select from the following frame settings:

1-2-3 displays the standard worksheet frame.

Enhanced displays a worksheet frame with lines highlighting the frame, each row, and column. This is the default worksheet frame in WYSIWYG.

Relief displays a sculpted worksheet frame, replaces the cyan color with gray, and turns brightness to high.

Menu Item	Function
	Special replaces the column letters and row numbers of the worksheet frame with horizontal and vertical rulers in the following way:
	Characters displays rulers in 10-point characters with six lines per inch; Inches displays rulers in inches; Metric displays rulers in centimeters; Points/Picas displays rulers in points and picas.
	None hides the worksheet frame.
Grid	Yes turns the worksheet grid lines on; No turns them off.
Page-Breaks	Yes displays page-break symbols; No hides them.
Cell-Pointer	Solid displays the cell pointer as a solid-colored rectangle. Outline displays it as a rectangular border around the current cell or range.
Intensity	Normal shows the display at normal intensity. High shows the display at high intensity.
Adapter	Lets you specify the graphics display adapter you want to use. Auto menu option is the default.
Quit	Returns you to the Display menu.

Display Quit

:DQ

Purpose

Returns 1-2-3 to READY mode.

To return to READY mode

    Type :DQ.

Display Rows

:DR

Purpose

    Specifies the number of rows that 1-2-3 displays on the screen while in graphics mode.

Reminder

    1-2-3 may display fewer or more rows than you specify; the number depends on the size of the default font and your graphics adapter card.

    1-2-3 can display from 16 to 60 rows. The default number depends on the display mode you selected during installation.

To choose the number of rows displayed

  1. Type :DR.

  2. Type a number from 16 to 60 and press Enter.

Display Zoom

:DZ

Purpose

    Enlarges or reduces the worksheet cells and affects the number of rows and columns that the screen can display.

To enlarge or reduce worksheet cells

  1. Type :DZ.

  2. Select one of the following commands:

Menu Item	Function
Tiny	Reduces cells to 63 percent of normal size.

Menu Item	Function
Small	Reduces cells to 87 percent of normal size.
Normal	Displays cells at normal size (100 percent).
Large	Enlarges cells to 125 percent of normal size.
Huge	Enlarges cells to 150 percent of normal size.
Manual	Reduces or enlarges cells according to a scale factor from 25 to 400. Type a number from 25 to 400 and press Enter.

Format Bold

:FB

Purpose

Changes data in a range from normal to bold or vice versa.

To make data bold

1. Type :FB.

2. Select Set to add bold to data in a range, or choose Clear to remove bold from data in a range.

3. Specify the cell or cell range.

Format Color

:FC

Purpose

Displays and prints cells or cell ranges in seven colors.

Reminder

You need a color monitor to display colors and a color printer to print colors.

To choose color text

1. Type :FC.

2. Select one of the following commands:

Menu Item	Function
Text	Changes the color of text in a range. Colors can be Normal, Red, Green, Dark-Blue, Cyan, Yellow, and Magenta.
Background	Changes the color of the background of a cell or cell range. Colors can be Normal, Red, Green, Dark-Blue, Cyan, Yellow, and Magenta.
Negative	Assigns a color for negative values in a range. Select Normal or Red.
Reverse	Switches the background and text colors in a range.
Quit	Returns 1-2-3 to READY mode.

3. Specify the cell or cell range.

Notes

Normal returns the color of the range to the color set with :Display Colors.

To display negative values in a color other than red, use :Display Colors Negative.

Format Font

Purpose

Changes the font of a cell or cell range, specifies the default font for a file, replaces fonts in the current font set, updates and restores the default font set, and saves font libraries in files on disk.

Reminder

You can use up to eight fonts in any file.

To select fonts

1. Type :FF.

2. Select one of the following commands:

Menu Item	Function
1 to 8	Changes the font of a cell or cell range to the numbered font after you specify the range.
Replace	Replaces one of the eight fonts in the current font set. 1 to 8 selects the font to replace. Swiss, Dutch, Courier, XSymbol, and Other selects a typeface. Enter a number from 3 to 72 to select a point size. Quit returns you to the Format Font menu.
Default	Restore replaces the current font set with the default font set. Update saves the current font set as the default font set.
Library	Determines factors regarding a font library file. Retrieve loads the font set you specify from those that you saved on disk previously. Save stores the current font set in a font library file on disk under the name

you specify. Erase deletes from disk
the font library file you specify.

Quit   Returns 1-2-3 to READY mode.

Notes

Fonts 1 to 8 comprise the current font set shown on the
screen when you select :Format Font.

1-2-3 saves the default font set in the WYSIWYG
subdirectory in the file FONTSET.CNF.

1-2-3 automatically adds the extension .AFS to font
libraries unless you enter a different extension.

Format Italics

:FI

Purpose

Changes data in a range from standard to italics or vice
versa.

To make data italic

1. Type :FI.

2. Select Set to add italics to data in a range or choose
   Clear to remove italics from data in a range.

3. Specify the cell or cell range.

Format Lines

:FL

Purpose

Draws single, double, or wide lines along the left, right,
top and bottom edges of cells or cell ranges, and adds a
drop shadow to cells or cell ranges.

To draw lines in your worksheet

1. Type :**FL**.

2. Select one of the following commands:

Menu Item	*Function*
Outline	Draws a single line around the edges of a cell or cell range.
Left	Draws a single vertical line along the left edge of a cell or cell range.
Right	Draws a single vertical line along the right edge of a cell or cell range.
Top	Draws a single horizontal line along the top edge of a cell or cell range.
Bottom	Draws a single horizontal line along the bottom edge of a cell or cell range.
All	Draws a single line around the edges of each cell in a range.
Double	Draws a double line where you specify. Select from **O**utline, **L**eft, **R**ight, **T**op, **B**ottom, and **A**ll.
Wide	Draws a thick line where you specify. Select from **O**utline, **L**eft, **R**ight, **T**op, **B**ottom, and **A**ll.
Clear	Removes lines from a cell or cell range as you specify. Select from **O**utline, **L**eft, **R**ight, **T**op, **B**ottom, and **A**ll.
Shadow	**S**et adds a drop shadow to a cell or cell range. **C**lear removes a drop shadow.

3. Specify the cell or cell range.

Format Quit

:FQ

Purpose
Returns 1-2-3 to READY mode.

To return to READY mode
Type :FQ.

Format Reset

:FR

Purpose
Removes all formatting from a cell or cell range, and returns font and color settings to the defaults that were set with the Display commands.

To return display settings to the defaults
1. Type :FR.
2. Specify the cell or cell range.

Note
:Format Reset does not affect formats set with /Range Format, /Worksheet Global Format, or the WYSIWYG formatting sequences.

Format Shade

:FS

Purpose
Adds light, dark, or solid shading to a range. Also removes shading from range.

Reminder
Solid shading hides the data in a range unless you use :Format Color Text to select another color for the data.

To add or remove shading from a range

1. Type :FS.

2. Select one of the following commands:

Menu Item	*Function*
Light	Adds light shading to a cell or cell range.
Dark	Adds dark shading to a cell or cell range.
Solid	Adds solid shading to a cell or cell range.
Clear	Removes shading from a cell or cell range.

3. Specify the cell or cell range.

Note

Solid shading prints in black, even if you have a color printer.

Format Underline

:FU

Purpose

Adds a single, double, or wide underline to a cell or cell range. Also removes underlining.

Reminder

Underlining appears only under data. It does not appear in blank cells or blank parts of a cell.

To use underlining

1. Type :FU.

2. Select one of the following commands:

Menu Item	Function
Single	Adds a single underline to a cell or cell range.
Double	Adds a double underline to a cell or cell range.
Wide	Adds a thick underline to a cell or cell range.
Clear	Removes underlining from a cell or cell range.

3. Specify the cell or cell range.

_____

Notes

Underlining is the same color as that selected with the :Display Colors Text command.

Use the :Format Lines command to underline blank cells.

Graph Add

:GA

_____

Purpose

Adds a graphic to the worksheet.

_____

To add a graphic

1. Type :GA.

2. Select one of the following commands:

Menu Item	Function
Current	Adds the current graph to the worksheet when you specify the single-sheet range in which you want the graphic to appear.

Menu Item	*Function*
Named	Adds a named graph from the current file to the worksheet when you specify a named graph from the current file, and then specify the single-sheet range in which you want the graph to appear.
PIC	Adds a 1-2-3 graph saved in a .PIC file to the worksheet when you specify a graph file with a .PIC extension, and then specify the single-sheet range in which you want the graph to appear.
Metafile	Adds a graphic saved in a .CGM file to the worksheet when you specify a file with a .CGM extension, and then specify the single-sheet range in which you want the graphic to appear.
Blank	Adds a blank graphic placeholder to the worksheet when you specify the single-sheet range in which you want the graphic to appear.

Notes

1-2-3 automatically sizes the graphic to fit in the specified range.

If you are designing a worksheet and know where you want to add a graphic but do not yet have the 1-2-3 graph or graphic metafile, use :Graph Add Blank to add a blank placeholder the size of the graphic you will eventually add. Later, you can use :Graph Settings Graph to replace the blank placeholder with the actual graphic.

Graph Compute

:GC

Purpose

Updates all graphics in the current worksheet.

To update your graphics

Type :**GC**.

Note

1-2-3 updates current and named 1-2-3 graphs and blank placeholders with every worksheet recalculation unless you change the default by selecting :**G**raph **S**ettings **S**ync **N**o.

Graph Edit

:GE

Purpose

Moves the graphics that you added to the worksheet with :Graph Add to the graphics editing window. You can then edit and enhance a graphic with the Graph Edit commands.

Reminder

You must be in Graphics Display mode to use the :**G**raph **E**dit commands.

You must select, or identify, objects and underlying graphics in the graphics editing window to edit, move, rearrange, or transform them with the :**G**raph **E**dit commands. You select objects with the :**G**raph **E**dit **S**elect commands or with the mouse.

To edit your graph

1. Type :**GE**.

2. Specify the graphic to edit by either specifying a cell in the range that the graphic occupies or by pressing **F3** (Name) and selecting the graphic from the list that 1-2-3 displays.

3. Select one of the following commands:

Menu Item	*Function*
Add	Adds objects such as text, geometric shapes, and freehand drawings to a graphic as follows:

Text adds letters, numbers, and special characters.

Line adds a single straight line or connected line segments.

Polygon adds an object with multi-sides.

Arrow adds a line segment or connected line segments with an arrowhead at one end.

Rectangle adds a rectangle.

Ellipse adds an ellipse or a circle.

Freehand adds a freehand drawing.

| Select | Selects a single object, a group of objects, or a graphic to edit in the graphics editing window: |

One selects a single object or the underlying graphic and deselects all other selected objects.

All selects all objects in the graphics editing window, but not the underlying graphic.

None deselects all selected objects and the underlying graphic.

More/Less selects or deselects objects or underlying graphics without affecting other selected objects.

Menu Item	*Function*
	Cycle selects or deselects objects and the underlying graphic by cycling through them one at a time. Use the cursor keys to cycle; press the **space bar** to toggle a selection; and press **Enter** to end the selection.
	Graph selects the underlying graphic.
	Quit returns you to the Graph Edit menu.
Edit	Changes the appearance of objects added to a graphic as follows:
	Text edits text added to a graphic with :Graph Edit Add.
	Centering left aligns, centers, or right aligns text added to a graphic with :Graph Edit Add.
	Font specifies a font for text added to a graphic with :Graph Edit Add. Press 1 to 8 to select the font.
	Line-Style changes lines or the outlines of rectangles, polygons, ellipses, or freehand drawings. Press 1 to 7 to select solid, dashed, dotted, long-dashed, chain-dotted, chain-dashed, or hidden lines.
	Width changes the thickness of lines or the outlines of rectangles, polygons, ellipses, or freehand drawings. Press 1 to 5 to select very narrow, narrow, medium, wide, or very wide lines.

Menu Item	*Function*
	Arrowheads adds arrowheads to lines and removes arrowheads from arrows. Switch moves the arrowhead to the other end of an arrow. One adds one arrowhead at the end of a line; Two adds arrowheads at both ends of lines or arrows. None removes arrowheads from an arrow.
	Smoothing replaces the angles of rectangles, polygons, freehand drawings, or connected line segments with curves. None removes smoothing from an object; Tight draws a smooth outline that approximates the original outline of an object. Medium draws an object with maximum smoothing.
Color	Specifies colors for a graphic and objects added to it as follows:
	Lines specifies a line or arrow's color, or the outline of a rectangle, polygon, ellipse, or freehand drawing. The color can be Black, White, Red, Green, Dark-Blue, Cyan, Yellow, Magenta, or Hidden.
	Inside specifies a color for the inside of a selected object. Select one of 224 colors that are displayed on-screen by typing the corresponding number and pressing Enter.
	Text specifies a color for text added to a graphic with :Graph Edit Add. Colors are Black, White, Red, Green, Dark-Blue, Cyan, Yellow, Magenta, or Hidden.

Menu Item	*Function*

Map changes up to 8 colors in the underlying graphic when you select a number from **1** to **8**. You then select one of 224 colors on the screen by typing the corresponding number. Press **Enter**.

Background specifies a color for the background of the range that the graphic occupies. Select one of 224 colors on the screen by typing the corresponding number. Press **Enter**.

Quit returns you to the Graph Edit menu.

Transform   Changes the orientation or size of a graphic and added objects added as follows:

Size changes the object size.

Rotate rotates the underlying graphic or selected objects at any angle around their axes.

Quarter-Turn rotates the underlying graphic or objects around their axes at 90-degree increments.

X-Flip flips objects horizontally.

Y-Flip flips objects vertically.

Horizontal adjusts the slant and size of objects by width.

Vertical adjusts the slant and size of objects by height.

Menu Item	*Function*

Clear cancels all :Graph Edit Transform commands and returns objects to their original states.

Rearrange   Copies, moves, deletes and restores, locks and unlocks, and determines the placement of objects added to a graphic as follows:

Delete removes selected objects from the graphics editing window.

Restore restores the most recently deleted objects to the graphics editing window.

Move moves selected objects within the graphics editing window.

Copy copies selected objects.

Lock protects selected objects from unwanted changes (the selection indicators of locked objects change from squares to diamonds).

Unlock removes the lock that protects objects from changes.

Front places objects in front of all other objects in the graphics editing window (objects in front may hide the objects in back of them).

Back places objects behind all other objects in the graphics editing window (objects in back may be hidden by objects in front of them).

View   Enlarges and reduces areas of the graphics editing window as follows:

Menu Item   *Function*

Full displays the contents of the graphics editing window at normal size.

In enlarges an area of the graphics editing window so that it fills the screen.

Pan permits you to use + and – to enlarge and reduce the contents of the graphics editing window. You can also use the pointer movement keys to move the display left, right, up, or down one-half screen in the graphics editing window.

+ enlarges the contents of the graphics editing window (you can select + up to five consecutive times).

– reduces the size of the contents of the graphics editing window (you can select – up to five consecutive times).

Up moves the display up one-half screen in the graphics editing window.

Down moves the display down one-half screen in the graphics editing window.

Left moves the display left one-half screen in the graphics editing window.

Right moves the display right one-half screen in the graphics editing window.

Menu Item	*Function*
Options	Grid No removes grid lines from the editing window display; Grid Yes adds grid lines.
	Cursor changes the size of the cursor in the graphics editing window. Small uses a small cross as the cursor; Big uses a large cross as the cursor.
	Font-Magnification changes the size of all text in a graphic, including text you add to a graph with 1-2-3 when you choose a number from 1 to 1000 to indicate the percentage change and press Enter.
Quit	Returns 1-2-3 to READY mode.

4. Many of these commands require moving a cursor that appears on the screen after a command is issued; use the pointer keys or mouse to move the cursor. Some commands require anchoring the cursor after moving it; use the **space bar** or left-hand mouse button to anchor the cursor. Press **Enter** or double-click the left-hand mouse button to complete an operation.

Notes

You can move a graphic to the graphics editing window any time 1-2-3 is in READY mode by double-clicking the graphic with the left mouse button.

To add the contents of a cell in an active file to a graphic with :Graph Edit Add Text, type \ (backslash) followed by the name or address of the cell. Press **Enter**. If you enter a range name or address, WYSIWYG adds the contents of the first cell in the range.

You can position an object you want to add to a graphic by using x-coordinates and y-coordinates as anchor points. Instead of using the mouse or pointer-movement

keys to move the cursor to a location, type *x,y* where *x* is
an x-coordinate from 0 to 4095 and *y* is a y-coordinate
from 0 to 4095.

Then, if you are adding a line of text or anchoring the
first point of a line, polygon, rectangle, ellipse, or
freehand drawing, click the left mouse button or press
the **space bar**.

If you are completing a line, polygon, rectangle, ellipse,
or freehand drawing, double-click the left mouse button
or press **Enter**.

Graph Goto

:GG

Purpose

Moves the cell pointer to a specific graphic in the
worksheet.

To move to a specific graph

1. Type **:GG**.

2. Type the name of the graphic, point to the name of
   the graphic, or type a cell address that lies within the
   range that the graphic occupies.

3. Press **Enter**.

Graph Move

:GM

Purpose

Moves a graphic to another range in the worksheet.

To move a graph

1. Type **:GM**.

2. Select the graphic to move by specifying a cell in the
   range that the graphic occupies or by pressing **F3**

(Name) and selecting the graphic from the list that
1-2-3 displays.

3. Specify the first cell of the new range for the graphic.

Notes

:Graph Move does not change the number of rows and
columns in the range that the graphic occupies. If you
move the graphic to a range with different row heights
or column widths, however, 1-2-3 automatically resizes
the graphic to fit in the new range.

:Graph Move does not affect any data that may be
underneath the graphic you move to another range.

Graph Quit

:GQ

Purpose

Returns 1-2-3 to READY mode.

To return to READY mode

Type :GQ.

Graph Remove

:GR

Purpose

Deletes a graphic from the worksheet.

Reminder

:Graph Remove does not delete the actual named graph,
graph file, graphic metafile, or current graph settings
from memory or from disk. Also, it does not affect any
data that may be underneath the graphic you delete from
the worksheet.

To delete a graph

1. Type :GR.

2. Select the graphic to remove by entering a cell
   address in the range that the graphic occupies or by
   pressing **F3** (Name) and selecting the graphic from
   the list that 1-2-3 displays.

3. Press **Enter**.

Notes

To specify more than one graphic to remove, specify a
range that contains more than one graphic.

If you delete a graphic from the worksheet with **:Graph
Remove**, you lose any enhancements you made to the
graphic with the **:Graph Edit** commands.

Graph Settings

:GS

Purpose

Moves and replaces graphics in the worksheet, turns the
display of graphics on or off, makes graphics in the
worksheet transparent or opaque, and makes 1-2-3
graphs in the worksheet update automatically when the
data on which the graphs are based changes.

To choose graph settings

1. Type **:GS**.

2. Select one of the following commands:

Menu Item	Function
Graph	Replaces a graphic in the worksheet with another graphic. Once you specify the graphic to replace, you may select one of the following choices:

Menu Item	*Function*
	Current replaces the specified graphic with the current graph.
	Named replaces the specified graphic with a named graph.
	PIC replaces the specified graphic with a 1-2-3 graph saved in a .PIC file.
	Metafile replaces the specified graphic with a graphic saved in a .CGM file.
	Blank replaces the specified graphic with a blank placeholder.
Range	Resizes the range a graphic occupies or moves a graphic in the worksheet to a specified range.
Sync	Controls whether a graph is updated automatically to reflect changes in the data on which it is based. Yes makes a named or current graph in the worksheet update these changes automatically; No turns off the feature.
Display	Yes displays a selected graphic in the worksheet; No displays a selected graphic as shaded rectangles in the worksheet.
Opaque	Yes hides worksheet data underneath a selected graphic; No makes worksheet data underneath a selected graphic visible.
Quit	Returns 1-2-3 to READY mode.

3. Select a graphic by specifying a cell in the range that the graphic occupies, or by pressing **F3** (Name) and selecting the graphic from the list that 1-2-3 displays. To specify more than one graphic, specify a range that contains more than one graphic.

4. Press **Enter**.

Notes

Resize a graphic, if desired, by using the mouse or pointer-movement keys to adjust the size of the range and pressing **Enter**.

To move a graphic to a range of the same size, use the **:G**raph **M**ove command.

Even if you turn off the display of a graphic in the worksheet, WYSIWYG still prints the actual graphic, not the shaded rectangle. Displaying a shaded rectangle instead of an actual graphic may improve speed because 1-2-3 does not have to redraw the graphic every time it recalculates or you move around the worksheet.

If you used **:G**raph **E**dit **C**olor **B**ackground to make the color of the range the graphic occupies transparent, 1-2-3 does not display anything in the worksheet when you select **:G**raph **S**ettings **D**isplay **N**o.

:Graph **S**ettings **G**raph does not remove any enhancements made with the Graph Edit commands. To replace a graphic and its enhancements, use **:G**raph **R**emove to remove the graphic and enhancements from the worksheet, then use **:G**raph **A**dd to add a different graphic.

When automatic recalculation of graphs is off, you must use **:G**raph **C**ompute to update current and named graphs in the worksheet.

Graph View

:GV

Purpose

Temporarily removes the worksheet from the screen and displays a graphic saved in a .PIC or .CGM file on the full screen.

To display a graph

1. Type :**GV**.

2. Select **P**IC to display a list of 1-2-3 graphs saved in .PIC files, or choose **M**etafile to display a list of graphics saved in .CGM files.

3. Select the graphic to display and press **Enter**.

4. When you finish viewing the graphic, press any key to remove it and redisplay the worksheet.

Graph Zoom

:GZ

Purpose

Temporarily removes the worksheet from the screen and displays a specified graphic in the worksheet on the full screen.

To display an enlarged view of a graph

1. Type :**GZ**.

2. Specify the graphic to display on the full screen by specifying a cell in the range the graphic occupies, or by pressing **F3** (Name) and selecting the graphic from the list 1-2-3 displays.

3. Press **Enter**.

4. When you finish viewing the graphic, press any key to redisplay the worksheet.

Named-Style

:N

Purpose

Defines a named style or collection of WYSIWYG formats taken from a single cell, and then applies it to one or more ranges in the current file.

Reminder

Each file can contain up to eight named styles.

To define a named style

1. Type :N.

2. Select one of the following commands:

Menu Item	Function
1-8	Formats one or more ranges with the named styles defined with :Named-Style Define.
Define	Creates a named style for the WYSIWYG formats in a specified cell.

3. Specify a cell or cell range.

4. For :Named-Style Define, type a name of up to six characters, type a description of up to 37 characters, and press **Enter**.

Note

If you redefine a named style, 1-2-3 automatically reformats any ranges formatted with that named style.

Print Background

:PB

Purpose

Prints data from an encoded file while allowing you to continue working in 1-2-3.

Reminder

Once the file has completed printing, 1-2-3 deletes the encoded file.

You must load the BPRINT utility program before you can use /Print Background. For more information, see "BPrint Utility" in Que's *Using 1-2-3 Rel. 2.3*.

To print from the background
1. Type :**PB**.
2. Define the print range with :**PR**.
3. Name the encoded file. If the file already exists, select **C**ancel to return to 1-2-3 without saving the file or select **R**eplace to write over the existing file.
4. Select **G**o.

Note

WYSIWYG uses printer codes specific to your current printer and enters them into the encoded file. You will only be able to print the encoded file on your current printer. You can also read an encoded file back into 1-2-3.

Print Config

:PC

Purpose

Specifies the printer, printer interface, font cartridges, orientation and paper-feed method.

To set up your printer
1. Type :**PC**.
2. Select one of the following commands:

Menu Item	*Function*
Printer	Selects the printer on which to print a specified range.
Interface	Specifies the interface, or port, that connects your computer to the printer when you select a number from **1** to **8**.
1st-Cart	Specifies a font cartridge or font card for your printer to use when you select a font-cartridge file or font-card file.

Menu Item	*Function*
2nd-Cart	Specifies a second font cartridge or font card for your printer to use when you select a second font-cartridge file or font-card file.
Orientation	Determines whether WYSIWYG prints in Portrait mode or Landscape mode, provided landscape mode is available on your printer.
Bin	Specifies the paper-feed option for your printer as follows:
	Reset clears the current bin setting.
	Single-Sheet selects a printer's single-sheet feeder.
	Manual selects a printer's continuous form-feed option.
	Upper-Tray selects a printer's top paper tray.
	Lower-Tray selects a printer's bottom paper tray.
Quit	Returns you to the Print menu.

Print File

:PF

Purpose

Prints a range to an encoded file. The file can include 1-2-3 data, graphics, and printer codes for all WYSIWYG options, such as fonts, colors, line spacing, and print compression. The printer codes WYSIWYG uses are specific to your current printer.

Reminder

You cannot read an encoded file back into 1-2-3.

To print to an encoded file

1. Specify a print range with :Print Range.

2. From the Print menu, select the File option.

3. Name the encoded file and press Enter.

4. If you are updating an existing encoded file, select Cancel to return 1-2-3 to READY mode without saving an encoded file or select Replace to write over the encoded file on disk with the current file.

Note

WYSIWYG automatically adds the extension .ENC to encoded files unless you specify a different extension.

Print Go

:PG

Purpose

Sends data to a printer.

To print your data

1. Specify a print range with :Print Range.

2. Check that the printer is on-line and the paper is at the top of a page.

3. From the Print menu, select Go.

Print Info

:PI

Purpose

Removes or redisplays the WYSIWYG print status screen that overlays the worksheet when you select :Print.

Reminder

1-2-3 removes the WYSIWYG print settings dialog box
if it is displayed, or displays the screen if it is not
displayed.

To remove or display the print status screen

Type :PI.

Note

You can also press F6 (WINDOW) to remove or display
the WYSIWYG print settings dialog box when you are
using the Print menu.

Print Layout

:PL

Purpose

Controls the page layout, or the overall positioning and
appearance of the page.

Reminder

1-2-3 saves page layout settings for a worksheet file in
that file's corresponding format file.

To set page appearance

1. Type :PL.

2. Select one of the following commands:

Command	Function
Page-Size	Specifies the length and width of the page when you select 1 to 7. Another option, Custom, permits you to enter a number manually for the page length and a number for the page width.

Command	Function
Margins	Sets Left, Right, Top, and Bottom margins when you enter a number followed by **in** or **mm** and press **Enter**; Quit returns you to the Print Layout menu.
Titles	Creates page headers and footers with the Header and Footer commands; clears them with the Clear Header, Clear Footer, or Clear Both commands; and returns to the Print Layout menu with the Quit command.
Borders	Specifies one or more rows to print at the top of every page and above every print range with the Top command; specifies one or more columns to print at the left of every page and print range with the Left command; clears these borders with the Clear Top, Clear Left, or Clear All commands; and returns to the Print Layout menu with the Quit command.
Compression	Compresses or expands a print range as follows:

None removes compression or expansion from a print range.

Manual compresses the print range when you type a number from **15** to **99** and press **Enter**. It expands the print range when you type a number from **101** to **1000** and press **Enter**.

Command	*Function*
	Automatic compresses a print range automatically, by up to a factor of seven, with the goal of fitting the range on one printed page whenever possible.
Default	Sets the default page layout. **U**pdate saves the current page layout settings as the default page layout setting; **R**estore replaces the current page layout settings with the default page layout settings.
Library	Enables you to **R**etrieve, **S**ave, or **E**rase page layout libraries on disk after you specify the name of the page layout library file. (Library files have .ALS extensions.)
Quit	Returns you to the Print menu.

3. If you select **:PLPC**, enter numbers in inches by typing the number followed by **"in"** and pressing **Enter**; enter numbers in millimeters by typing the number followed by **"mm"** and pressing **Enter**.

    If you select **:PLTH** or **:PLTF**, type the header or footer at the prompt and press **Enter**.

    If you select **:PLBT** or **:PLBL**, specify a range that includes the rows or columns you want to use as a border.

    If you select **:PLLS** to update an existing layout library, select **C**ancel to return 1-2-3 to READY mode without saving the current layout library or select **R**eplace to write over the layout library on disk with the current layout library.

Notes

Type **CM** to denote a setting in centimeters; WYSIWYG automatically converts the setting to millimeters.

Combined left and right margin settings cannot be greater than the width of the paper. Combined top and bottom margin settings cannot be greater than the length of the paper.

Do not include in your print range the rows and columns you specified as borders, or WYSIWYG prints those rows and columns twice.

WYSIWYG prints headers on the line below the top margin and footers on the line above the bottom margin. WYSIWYG always leaves two blank lines, measured in the default font, between printed data and the header or footer.

WYSIWYG uses four symbols to format headers and footers: # (pound sign) for page numbers, @ (at sign) for the current date, | (vertical bar) for alignment, and \ (backslash) to copy cell contents.

Print Preview

:PP

Purpose

Temporarily removes the worksheet from the screen and displays the print range as WYSIWYG will format it for printing, page by page.

To preview the print job

1. Type **:PP**.

2. Press any key except **Esc** to cycle through the pages; press **Esc** to redisplay the worksheet.

Print Quit

:PQ

Purpose

Returns 1-2-3 to READY mode.

To return to READY mode

Type :PQ.

Print Range

:PR

Purpose

Specifies or cancels the print range, which is the data that WYSIWYG prints when you select :Print Go or :Print File.

Reminder

The print range can include any number of ranges in the current file.

To specify or cancel a print range

1. Type :PR.

2. Select Set to specify the print range; select Clear to clear the settings for the current print range.

3. If you select Set, specify the print range to set and press Enter.

Notes

If the print range includes a long label, include in the print range the cells that the long label overlaps as well as the cell in which you entered the long label.

In Graphics Display mode, the boundaries of the print range appear as dashed lines along the edges of the print range. The dashed lines remain on the screen until you clear the print range with :Print Range Clear.

Print Settings

:PS

Purpose

Specifies which pages of a print range to print, the number of copies to print, whether to print the worksheet frame and grid lines, and whether to pause for manual paper feed. The :Print Settings command also controls page numbering.

Reminder

The WYSIWYG print settings are separate from the 1-2-3 print settings and, except for the Frame and Grid settings, affect only the current WYSIWYG session. You can use Frame and Grid over and over again without resetting them.

To choose print settings

1. Type :PS.

2. Select one of the following commands:

Menu Item	Function
Begin	Specifies the number of the page at which to begin printing.
End	Specifies the last page to print.
Start-Number	Specifies the page number of the first page in the print range.
Copies	Specifies the number of copies to print.
Wait	Specifies if the printing pauses after each page. No does not pause printing after each page; Yes pauses printing after each page.
Grid	Specifies if worksheet grid lines are printed with the print range. No does not print worksheet grid lines; Yes prints worksheet grid lines.

Menu Item	Function
Frame	Specifies if the worksheet frame is printed with the print range. No does not print the worksheet frame; Yes prints the worksheet frame.
Reset	Returns the WYSIWYG print settings to the defaults.
Quit	Returns you to the Print menu.

3. If you select B, E, S, or C, type the appropriate number and press Enter.

    If you select :PSWY, WYSIWYG gives you time to insert the next sheet of paper before you press any key to resume or press Esc to cancel.

Notes

The beginning and ending page numbers depend on the page numbering you specify with :Print Settings Start-Number.

WYSIWYG prints the standard 1-2-3 worksheet frame regardless of how you choose to display the worksheet frame with :Display Options Frame.

 Quit _____

:Q

Purpose

Returns 1-2-3 to READY mode.

To return to READY mode

Type :Q.

Special Copy

:SC

Purpose

Copies all WYSIWYG formats in one range to another
range

Reminder

:Special Copy does not copy data, graphics in the
worksheet, or 1-2-3 formats that you set with the /Range
Format or /Worksheet Global Format commands.

To copy WYSIWYG formats

1. Type :SC.

2. Specify the range from which you want to copy
   formats and press Enter.

3. Specify the range to which you want to copy formats
   and press Enter.

Special Export

:SE

Purpose

Saves the font set, formats, named styles, and graphics
in a WYSIWYG format file (.FMT).

To save a WYSIWYG format file

1. Type :SE.

2. Specify a format file to which to export and press
   Enter.

3. If you are updating an existing format file, select
   Cancel to return 1-2-3 to READY mode without
   exporting the current format file; select Replace to
   write over the format file on disk with a copy of the
   current format file.

Notes

1-2-3 automatically exports to a WYSIWYG format file
(.FMT) unless you enter a different extension. To export
to an Allways format file, enter the extension **.ALL** after
the file name.

If the file from which you export contains current or
named graphs, 1-2-3 exports only their positions in the
worksheet and enhancements made with the :Graph Edit
commands, not the graphs themselves.

Many WYSIWYG features are not available in Allways
and are therefore lost when you try to save them in an
Allways format file (.ALL).

Special Import

:SI

Purpose

Applies the formats, named styles, font set, and graphics
from a WYSIWYG format file (.FMT) or Allways
format file (.ALL) on disk to the current file.

Reminder

1-2-3 automatically imports from a WYSIWYG format
file (.FMT) unless you enter a different extension. To
import from an Allways format file, enter the extension
.ALL after the file name.

To import a format file

1. Type **:SI**.

2. Select one of the following commands:

Menu Item	Function
All	Replaces all formats, named styles, and graphics in the current file with the formats, named styles, and graphics from a format file on disk.

Menu Item	Function
Named-Styles	Replaces the named styles in the current file with the named styles from a WYSIWYG or Allways format file on disk.
Fonts	Replaces the font set in the current file with the font set from a format file on disk.
Graphs	Copies graphics, including their positions in the worksheet and all enhancements added with the :Graph Edit commands, from a format file on disk to the current file.

3. Specify a format file from which to import and press **Enter**.

Notes

:Special Import Graphs does not delete any graphic that you already added to the current file with :Graph Add.

If you import current or named graphs, 1-2-3 imports only their positions in the worksheet and enhancements made with the Graph Edit commands, not the graphs themselves.

Special Move

:SM

Purpose

Transfers the format of one range to another range and causes the cells that originally contained the formats to revert to the default formats. This command does not move data, graphics, or 1-2-3 formats set with the /Range Format or /Worksheet Global Format commands.

To move a range format

1. Type :SM.

2. Specify the range from which you want to move formats and press Enter.

3. Specify the range to which you want to move formats and press Enter.

Text Align

:TA

Purpose

Changes the alignment of labels within a text range by changing their label prefixes.

To change label prefixes in a range

1. Type :TA.

2. Select one of the following:

Menu Item	Function
Left	Aligns labels with the left edge of the text range.
Right	Aligns labels with the right edge of the text range.
Center	Centers labels in the text range.
Even	Aligns labels with both the left and right edges of the text range.

3. Specify the range within which you want to align labels. Press Enter.

Text Clear

:TC

Purpose

Clears the settings for a text range, but does not erase the data contained in the range or change any formatting performed on the data using the **:Text Reformat** or **:Text Edit** commands.

To clear text range settings

1. Type **:TC**.

2. Specify the text range whose settings you want to clear and press **Enter**.

Text Edit

:TE

Purpose

Enables you to enter and edit labels in a text range directly in the worksheet instead of in the control panel.

To enter and edit labels in a range

1. Type **:TE**.

2. Specify the range in which you want to edit text and press **Enter**.

3. When you finish editing, press **Esc** to return 1-2-3 to READY mode.

Note

When you issue the **:Text Edit** command, a cursor appears at the first character in the range and the mode indicator changes to TEXT.

Text Reformat

:TR

Purpose

Rearranges (justifies) a column of labels so that the
labels fit within a text range.

Reminders

Before using the command, you first must select
:Display Mode Graphics. To use :Text Reformat, you
must turn off global protection for the worksheet that
contains the column of labels.

Using :Text Reformat on cells whose contents are used
in formulas may change or invalidate the results of the
formulas.

To justify labels to fit a text range

1. Move the cell pointer to the first cell in the column of
   labels you want to rearrange.

2. Type :TR.

3. Specify the text range in which you want to rearrange
   labels and press Enter.

Notes

:Text Reformat affects labels in only the first column of
a text range.

When WYSIWYG rearranges the text, it aligns all of the
labels within the range depending on the first label's
label prefix.

Text Set

:TS

Purpose

Specifies a text range so that you can use the Text
commands with labels in the range.

To specify a text range for Text commands

1. Type :TS.

2. Specify the range that you want to make a text range and press Enter.

Worksheet Column

:WC

Purpose

Sets the width of one or more columns and resets columns to the 1-2-3 global column width.

Reminder

The column widths that you specify remain in effect even after you remove WYSIWYG from memory.

To set column width

1. Type :WC.

2. Select Set-Width to set the column width for one or more columns; select Reset-Width to reset one or more columns to the global column width.

3. If you selected Set-Width, specify the range of columns whose widths you want to set. Specify the new width either by typing a number from 1 to 240 and pressing Enter, or by using the ← or → keys and pressing Enter.

   If you selected Reset-Width, specify the range of columns whose widths you want to reset to the global column width and press Enter.

Notes

When the screen is split into two horizontal or vertical windows, the :Worksheet Column commands affect only the window in which the cell pointer is located. When you clear the windows, 1-2-3 uses the top or left window's column settings.

If you set the display of your worksheet frame with
:Display Options Frame Enhanced or :Display Options
Frame Relief, you can use the mouse to set the width of
a column whenever 1-2-3 is in READY mode. You can
also use the mouse to hide or redisplay a column
whenever 1-2-3 is in READY mode.

Worksheet Page

:WP

Purpose

Inserts or removes horizontal or vertical page breaks that
tell 1-2-3 to begin a new page when printing with the
WYSIWYG :Print commands.

To insert or remove page breaks

1. Position the cell pointer in the leftmost column or top
   row on which you want a new page to start.

2. Type :WP.

3. Select one of the following commands:

Menu Item	Function
Row	Inserts a horizontal page break.
Column	Inserts a vertical page break.
Delete	Removes vertical and/or horizontal page breaks from the current column and/or row.
Quit	Returns 1-2-3 to READY mode.

Notes

1-2-3 inserts a dashed line along the left of the column
for a vertical page break or along the top of the row for a
horizontal page break. When you print your data, 1-2-3
starts a new page at the row or column you specified.

To hide the dashed lines that symbolize page breaks on
your screen, use :Display Options Page-Breaks No.

Worksheet Row

:WR

Purpose

Sets the height of one or more rows. You can specify a height in points, or make 1-2-3 automatically set row heights to accommodate the largest font in a row.

Procedures

1. Type :WR.

2. Select Set-Height to set the row height for one or more rows; select Auto to automatically set the height of one or more rows based on the size of the largest font in the row.

3. If you select Set-Height, specify the range of rows whose heights you want to set. You can then specify the row height, either by typing a number from 1 to 255 and pressing Enter or by using the up- and down-arrow keys and pressing Enter.

   If you select Auto, specify the range of rows whose heights you want 1-2-3 to set automatically and press Enter.

Note

If you set the display of your worksheet frame with :Display Option Frame Enhanced or :Display Options Frame Relief, you can use the mouse to set the height of a row whenever 1-2-3 is in READY mode. You can also use the mouse to hide or redisplay a row whenever 1-2-3 is in READY mode.

Index

sorting databases, 31-32
splitting worksheet windows, 83
square matrices, 25
stacked-bar graphs, 47
Step (Alt-F2) function key, 5
STEP mode, 89-90
suppressing zeros, 79-80

T

Table (F10) function key, 4
tables, 34
    creating, 68
    files, 34
    generating, 32
text
    aligning, 77
    boldfacing, 103
    justifying, 66-67
    searching, 69-70
transposing data, 70
types of graphs, 47-48
type styles
    bold, 103
    italic, 106

U

underlining, 109-110
Undo (Alt-F4) function key, 5
unprotected cells, 66, 68-69
updating graphics in worksheets, 112

V

values
    combining, 34-35
    copying, 22
    defining defaults, 76-77
    moving, 49
    replacing in formulas, 70
viewing
    files, 57, 94-95
    graphs, 124-125

W

Window (F6) function key, 4
windows
    creating with mouse, 7
    splitting, 83
worksheets
    adding graphics, 110-111
    checking statuses, 82
    defining
        areas to be printed, 56
        calculations, 78-79
        columns/rows, 72
    deleting graphs, 121
    displaying colors, 96-97
    displaying rows, 102
    drawing lines, 106-107
    enlarging/reducing display, 102-103
    erasing, 73
    hiding columns, 71-72
    inserting columns/rows, 80
    inserting page breaks while
        printing, 82
    loading, 37
    moving, 120-124
    printing, 49-52
    protecting, 77
    saving, 38-39
    selecting portions to be printed, 56
    setting column widths, 73, 143
    setting row height, 145
    splitting, 83
    updating graphics, 112
WYSIWYG, 95
    defining named styles, 125-126
    displaying colors for worksheets,
        96-97
    loading into memory, 95
    saving settings, 137

X-Z

x-axis, 39-40, 45
XY graphs, 47
y-axis, 39-40, 45
zeros, 79-80